PROTECTIONIST REPUBLICANISM

Also by Clarence A. Stern:

GOLDEN REPUBLICANISM:
THE CRUSADE FOR HARD MONEY

REPUBLICAN HEYDAY: REPUBLICANISM
THROUGH THE MCKINLEY YEARS

RESURGENT REPUBLICANISM:
THE HANDIWORK OF HANNA

PROTECTIONIST REPUBLICANISM

Republican Tariff Policy
in the
McKinley Period

By Clarence A. Stern, Ph.D.

Copyright © 1971 by Clarence A. Stern

Library of Congress Catalog Card Number: 70-135167
SBN 0-9600116-4-1

Lithographed in U.S.A. by

EDWARDS
BROTHERS
INCORPORATED
2500 SOUTH STATE STREET / ANN ARBOR, MICHIGAN 48104

TO
KATHLEEN

FOREWORD

Significant in its relation to such aspects of McKinley-era Republican policy as those involved in the trust problem, the monetary question, and imperialism was the protective tariff. Generally regarded by leading Republicans as the most vital principle of their policy, protectionism contributed to party cohesion, served as a publicity-gaining vehicle for aspiring politicos, and promoted the party's alliance with industrialists highly influential in shaping the course of governmental action.

Although enlisting a measure of support from the Democrats, long plagued by Republican charges of wartime disloyalty, protectionism received its principal backing from the professedly unimpeachable Party of the Union, vociferously characterized by its protagonists as eternally committed to love of country and the perpetuation of the nation-state. In their exaggerated appeals for tariff rate-escalation, Republican leaders portrayed protectionism as an agent of prosperity, capable of providing benefits for all, including workingmen and farmers, and as a policy conducive to the development of virtue and patriotism. During a period of emerging industrialism in which the "bloody shirt" issue was gradually being replaced by that of the tariff as the most prominent feature of Republican policy, protectionism reflected the resolute effort of party leaders to render the government increasingly responsive to the interests of big business.

In the Republican drive for ever higher tariff duties

was apparent the industrialist influence permeating a restricted concept of political leadership. Contributing to the growing harmony of the party and to its improving efficiency as a vote-garnering machine were the augmented financial resources available to Republican leaders increasingly inclined to view the G.O.P. as primarily a business-enterprise-promotion agency dedicated to the determination of tariff schedules by the protectionist beneficiaries themselves. Mirrored in the Republican rate-escalation triumphs culminating in the unprecedentedly high Dingley tariff act were the ardent labors of such eminent figures as Mark Hanna, William McKinley, Thomas B. Reed, John Sherman, and Nelson W. Aldrich.

Of fundamental significance in the emergence and effectiveness of the Hanna-McKinley team was its identification with ultra-protectionism. Hanna selected McKinley for intended presidential service chiefly on the basis of his reputation as the most conspicuous advocate of high tariffs. Hanna's abiding belief in the sanctity of the protective system constituted probably the most dynamic and enduring element in the extraordinarily successful arrangement between the millionaire-industrialist-turned-politician and the longtime professional politician in need of a Warwick. Reflected in McKinley's ascent to the White House and in his hasty direction of executive authority to the support of the Dingley tariff legislation was protectionist vindication of the president-making project so assiduously pursued by the "business man in politics." In successfully applying his industrialist-based power to the grooming, guiding, and safeguarding of a high-tariff-minded protege desperately requiring assistance for the preservation of his presidential eligibility, Hanna furthered, and was aided by, the potent force of ultra-protectionism.

Highlighting the protectionist services of Reed, Sherman, and Aldrich were activities singularly attuned to their aptitudes as leading Republican legislators. Speaker Reed, in combining his high-tariff zeal with his proficiency as parliamentarian in arrogantly forcing through a revolutionary revision of the House rules, brought the traditionally filibuster-ridden lower chamber to the support of his party and thus opened the way for favorable action on the McKinley bill. Senator Sherman's capability as compromiser came into play in his promotion, during a period of inter-sectional strife over the currency and tariff issues, of a conservatively oriented agreement providing for the passage of the McKinley measure and of legislation for the limited purchase of silver. The aristocratic Senator Aldrich, well known for his narrowly economic interpretation of his official duties, and credited with having done more than any other legislator in the preparation of the 1890 tariff bill, won infinite admiration and undying praise from industrialists deeply impressed by his demonstration of devotion and consummate skill in advancing their interests.

Discernible in the growing disposition of Republican leaders to view their organization as a business-fostering agency was the rising influence of the managers of corporate wealth in the operation of the party. During a period which witnessed, partly because of civil-service-reform legislation prohibiting political assessments upon office holders, a shift to corporate contributions as the major source of the party's revenue, the increasingly generous donors were accorded, in recompense for their swelling financial assistance, predominance in the formation of Republican policy. Indicative of the emerging domination of the party by the corporate managers was the

Hanna-guided transformation of the astonishingly affluent organization into an efficient vote-garnering mechanism not given to scrupulousness about corruption.

Reflecting the protectionist pro-business bias was the Republican view concerning the permissible extent of governmental authority within the sphere of industrialist activity. The application of such power, party leaders maintained, could be regarded as tolerable only when directed to the welfare of the manufacturing and commercial classes. Espoused by protectionist Republicans was a type of laissez-faire economic philosophy conceding a plenitude of governmental power for intervention in the operation of the highly esteemed free-enterprise system through the imposition of tariff duties for the enrichment of industrialists. Precluded from the Republican concept of sufferable governmental action was any assumption that a sovereign nation-state could implement effective trust-regulating legislation or exercise the taxing power for the purpose of procuring from the wealthy classes a more equitable share of the federal revenue.

Partly as a consequence of the fervent endorsement of tariff rate-elevation as the principal objective of the McKinley-era Republican party, its approach to the task of governing was essentially devoid of enlightened solicitude for the overall national interest. In their insistence upon equating the general welfare with that of the tariff-benefiting industrialists, the Republican leaders would appear to have manifested faith in protectionism as a panacea obviating any need for realistic consideration of the national welfare. Despite occasional acknowledgment by high-tariff advocates that the protective system was really intended mainly for the benefit of the favored indus-

trialists, and notwithstanding the admission by some
ultra-protectionists that duties had indeed been driven
too high, the rate-escalation crusade served as a de-
terrent to the development of Republican concern for
the general welfare.

Contributing to the retention of power by the Republicans during the period under consideration despite the faulty perspective apparent in their approach
to governing the nation was the weakness of the Democratic party. That agrarian oriented organization,
flouted by persisting charges of treasonable conduct
and hampered by a dearth of financial resources,
proved incapable of providing serious competition for
the effective control of the government. Aggravating
the shortcomings of the Democratic party were the
essential similarity of its policy to that of the G.O.P.,
and the disintegrating effect of President Cleveland's
inept leadership. In his disappointing retreat from
tariff-reform, and in his wilful sacrifice of party
unity upon the altar of the gold standard, Cleveland
demonstrated a strongly pro-industrialist posture
highly welcome to protectionist Republicans. Free
from any opposition-party pressure that might con-
ceivably have promoted the development of construc-
tive leadership within their own ranks, the Republicans
could conveniently concentrate upon protectionism as
the easy road of least resistance.

Highlighted by the Republican pre-occupation with
the welfare of the industrialists was a profusion of
political expediency featuring an avid desire to please
the managers of corporate wealth through the continuing escalation of tariff rates. At the helm of the
copiously financed and increasingly efficient Republican organization sat the tariff-enriched captains of
industry. Involved in the fervid solicitude for industrialist welfare was the view of tariff rate-escalation

as a panacea, an outlook detrimental to the development of leadership dedicated to the provision of enlightened government for the nation as a whole. In burdening the country with a plethora of protectionism, the McKinley-era Republicans demonstrated their unconcern for the development of leadership geared to the promotion of the national interest.

CONTENTS

PROTECTION FOR INDUSTRIALISTS:
THE POST-CIVIL WAR YEARS

Long regarded as a necessity by captains of industry, the protective tariff attained, during the McKinley era, a dominant position as the keystone of Republican policy, and as such claimed the earnest attention of ambitious party leaders.[1] So influential did the protectionists become that duties were pushed, under Republican leadership, to extremely high levels. The protective principle, utilized with moderation as a part of Hamilton's financial program in 1789, and applied on a decreasing scale in the period immediately prior to the Civil War,[2] came to be so intensively practiced as to raise doubts even on the part of McKinley as to whether rates had not been thrust too high. Accelerated by the demands of industrialists, the movement for increased duties was not impeded by the half-hearted objections of such professed exponents of moderation as Senators John Sherman and William Boyd Allison.

The protectionists, losing little time following the accession of the Republican party to power in 1861, succeeded, with the passage of the Morrill tariff act of that year, in effecting a reversal of the earlier downward trend. This measure did not constitute war legislation and did not reflect any general demand on the part of manufacturers for increased duties.[3]

However, the outbreak of the Civil War introduced economic and political circumstances which served the purpose of protectionist Republicans in their effort to make additional increases in the tariff. Aiding

1

these partisans in the pursuit of this objective were
the wartime requirements for additional revenue and
the growing clamor of manufacturers for higher duties
to offset the internal taxes on domestic industries.
These developments, coupled with the virtual cessa-
tion of anti-tariff sentiment in Congress resulting
from secession, enabled the dominant Republicans to
enact successively higher tariff measures in 1862 and
1864.[4]

Nor did the termination of the costly conflict bring
the tariff reduction generally promised when the wartime revenue measures were enacted. Only tempo-
rarily successful were the efforts of David A. Wells,
special revenue commissioner, and of Western Congressmen in effecting slight decreases in the acts of
1870 and 1872. Progress in the direction of reduced
duties was halted by the tariff law of 1875, which re-
scinded the ten per cent horizontal reduction provided
three years earlier.[5]

Although the post-Civil War period witnessed the
repeal of most of the internal revenue duties imposed
during the conflict,[6] the Republican-dominated Congress of the reconstruction era obstructed all
attempts at similar action in regard to tariff duties.[7]
In support of the postwar refusal of the Republican
legislators to provide the widely expected tariff reform stood the highly favored industrialists. They
came, in recognition of the tremendous advantages
afforded by the war duties, to regard protection as a
profitable "vested interest." It was in the light of "a
national commitment" to themselves that the perpetuation of protectionist policy was regarded by manufacturers who had prospered under the system.[8]

Among the Republican leaders who served the interests of industrialists by supporting increased
tariffs were William McKinley, Nelson W. Aldrich,

John Sherman, William Boyd Allison, Benjamin Harrison, and Thomas B. Reed. Most enthusiastic and persistent in their protectionist endeavors were McKinley and Aldrich. Less zealous but highly instrumental in contributing to the enactment of successively higher tariff measures were Sherman and Allison. These two mid-Westerners, despite their predilections for moderation in the application of protection, chose to regard themselves as bound by the compulsions of party regularity to support the high tariff bills emerging as Republican measures. As for Harrison and Reed, they too assisted in meeting the protectionist demands of manufacturers and in according to the protective principle a position of major significance in the formation of Republican policy.

In the forefront of the party from the standpoint of attaining widespread and enduring publicity through the preaching of the protectionist doctrine was William McKinley. Moved by a deep and long-abiding devotion to high tariffs,[9] this amiable son and grandson of iron manufacturers, industrialists who relied heavily upon tariff duties,[10] early dedicated himself to the promotion of the principle which he embraced with heart and soul. From 1876, when he was first elected to the House as Representative of Ohio's 17th district, McKinley directed his energies, his personal charm, and his undoubted political acumen to the task of providing industry with what he regarded as its just desert,[11] namely, high tariff duties.

McKinley, convinced of "the infallibility of protection," believed that "there could not be too much of it," and so "he could with clear conscience give all that the manufacturer asked, and then add a little, confident that he was really fostering prosperity."[12] The conscientious manner in which he followed the example of "Pig Iron" Kelley[13] had resulted, with the failing health of that Pennsylvania Representative, in the filling of his place by McKinley.[14] Long before Garfield's resignation from Congress upon his assumption of presidential duties, at which time McKinley emerged as "the acknowledged leader of the protectionist group,"[15] he had in his speech against the Wood tariff reduction bill exuberantly expounded his faith.[16]

In this House speech of April 15, 1878, an orthodox tariff message intended to comfort Kelley,[17] McKinley presented arguments which he would frequently reiterate in subsequent efforts to stave off tariff reductions and to secure upward revision of duties. The proposed measure, he asserted, would, if enacted, be "a public calamity" and would injure "the mining, the manufacturing, and the industrial classes of this country." As in his view the mere discussion of the tariff question constituted "a terror to the commercial classes," he advocated delay.

To McKinley any substantial tariff revision represented "a delicate and hazardous undertaking" requiring great caution. The immediate enactment of the pending measure, he warned, "would be an act of criminality." The defeat of the Wood bill McKinley declared to be "the dictate of every just principle of morals and fair dealing." A "high moral right," he averred, rested upon Congress "to still further the protection which in the past has been given to the industries of the country."

In regard to the alleged benefits of protectionist legislation McKinley in this 1878 House speech called attention to the encouragement of industrial expansion, the enhancement of the value of real estate, the creation of a market for farm products, and the provision of employment for laborers. In presenting the pauper labor argument he admitted that current wages were inadequate but claimed to see in the Wood bill the "inevitable reduction of the price of labor" throughout the nation. He protested against any legislation which would result in the lowering of wages, and he declared that in the event of diminution of duties labor would be "the first to suffer."

Although McKinley expressly denied that prohibition of importation was a part of the American system, he declared that "self-preservation is the first law of nature, as it should be of nations." Legislation which did not encourage industry and labor, he asserted, was "in opposition to the great law of life, and subversive of the principles upon which governments are established."

In this address of April 15, 1878 Representative McKinley regarded the "general welfare" as identical with the encouragement of domestic industry and labor. The protective tariff would increase the national wealth and would benefit farmers and laborers as well as industrialists, he held. His plea for the continuation of protection was colored by the spirit of laissez faire. "Above all else," declared McKinley, the nation "at this critical period" wanted "rest—rest from legislation, safety and security as to its basis of business, certainty as to the resources of the Government, immunity from legislative tinkering."

In his endeavor to assure the continued acceptance by Republican policy makers of his protectionist philosophy, McKinley followed a course which gained for him nation-wide attention and thus contributed to his availability as a candidate for the presidency. His aid in the obstruction of tariff reform, his participation in the "Great Debate" over the Mills bill in 1888, and the widespread use of his name in the publicizing of the unprecedentedly high tariff act of 1890 com-

bined to increase his prominence as a leading spokesman for the cause of extreme protection.

As a member of the Ways and Means Committee,
McKinley co-operated in the congressional maneuvers
directed toward avoiding tariff reduction at the hands
of those who favored such action as a method of decreasing the treasury surplus.[18] Among his activities
aimed at holding the strong position already attained
and at achieving greater protectionist gains in the
future was his delivery of a speech in the House on
April 6, 1882.[19] In this address he supported a measure providing for the appointment by President
Arthur of a non-congressional commission representing industry, commerce, and agriculture, to be
charged with the task of making recommendations
regarding tariff reform.[20]

Though McKinley conceded the possibility of some
need for slight modification of duties, he stated that
"general revision" could "well be left for many years
to come." He had "no fear," however, "of an intelligent and business-like examination and revision of
the tariff by competent civilians, who shall be known
Americans, favorable to the American system." In
the course of this 1882 House address, comprising
another extended exposition of the manifold advantages of high duties, McKinley stressed the view that
far from being confined to manufacturers, protectionist benefits reached farmers and laborers. To
"the protective system that was enacted by the Republican party" he attributed what he regarded as the
high living standard of American workmen.[21]

Whatever the tariff commission could recommend
that was good, Representative McKinley had stated in
his speech of April 6, 1882, could be accepted by Congress, but any recommendations not subject to such
description, he added, could and would be rejected.

And it was in line with this outlook that he and his fellow protectionists chose to reject the major portion of the recommendations issued by the commission whose members suggested an average reduction ranging from 20 to 25 per cent.[22]

Obviously displeased with what they regarded as unwarranted irreverence toward their dogma, the apostles of protection were successful in limiting to 5 per cent the average decrease of rates in the act of March 3, 1883.[23] Shadows were cast upon the validity of even this nominal reduction because of the inclusion in the measure of frequently concealed increases designed to benefit the steel, cotton, and wool manufacturers. Though duties were decreased on articles not involved in the import trade, rates were augmented on commodities in competition with domestic production. Thus the tariff law of 1883 constituted a protectionist triumph.[24]

This high tariff victory, though due in part to a lack of unity among the Democrats on this issue,[25] was to a large extent ascribable to the labors of such experienced and capable Republicans as Senators Aldrich, Allison, and Sherman. In no way detracting from the important role played by McKinley in making the act of 1883 a protectionist success[26] was the fact that the interests of industrialists were being effectively promoted by a rising young solon, Nelson W. Aldrich of Rhode Island.

From the time of his admission to the Senate in 1881,[27] Aldrich, whose undisguised economic concept of his legislative duties[28] assured him of uninterrupted support by his politically stable industrial constituency, was regarded by his colleagues as "a coming man."[29] Scornful of the public,[30] but highly concerned over the welfare of his industrialist supporters, he rapidly revealed himself as one of the ablest exponents of extreme protection. His reputation for excelling in committee service he earned in connection with the preparation and enactment of the tariff legislation of 1883. Though not without skill as a tactician and debater in open meetings, Aldrich, whom his biographer chooses to describe as "the sphinx at the back of the Republican policies,"[31] preferred the more private atmosphere of closed conferences, committees, and caucuses.[32]

As a member both of the Senate Finance Committee and of the conference committee which gave final form to the high tariff act of 1883, Aldrich found extensive scope for his ability to shape legislation favorable to the manufacturing interests. Steffens, who refers to Aldrich as the spokesman for "protected, that is to say, privileged business," observes that "it was as the representative of the manufacturers of his state that he felt bound to make himself an authority on tariff legislation."[33]

Aldrich not only frankly acknowledged his industrialist sympathies,[34] but he displayed unexcelled knowledge of factual data and a lack of prejudice against the application of complicated classifications and schedules. He readily drew attention to himself as providing an unusual degree of assistance to his colleagues on the Finance Committee while at the same time rendering especially effective service to the woolen, cotton, and sugar industries.[35] On the Senate floor, also, through the outstanding skill with which he frequently explained intricate provisions of the tariff bill of 1883, he proved of inestimable value to the less capable chairman of the Finance Committee, Senator Morrill, and to the protectionist cause as well.[36]

As if to make certain that a project well under way from the protectionist standpoint should not be allowed to lag in its final phase, Aldrich served as a member of the conference committee. This group, whose operation has been described as "one of the obscurities of tariff history,"[37] managed to amend the measure "in a protectionist direction,"[38] thereby performing the feat of practically "leaving the tariff where it was."[39] Aldrich later justified the action of the conference committee by contending that the bill as passed made no actual increase in the tariff and that the modifications approved by the committee resulted from the convincing nature of requests on the part of representatives of industries.[40]

Such solicitude for the manufacturers as was demonstrated by Aldrich in connection with the tariff act of 1883 could hardly be expected to be overlooked by industrialists pressing their demands for the imposition of high tariff duties. The commercial interests were appreciative, as well as aware, of the unique talent involved in his unflinching and highly successful promotion of the protectionist cause. From the time of Senator Aldrich's effective contribution to the passage of the measure of 1883 "business men interested in tariffs had come to count on him more and more."[41]

Prominent among the Republican congressional leaders who though possessed of less extreme tariff views than those held by McKinley and Aldrich nevertheless supported the act of 1883 and subsequent protectionist measures were Senators Sherman of Ohio and Allison of Iowa.[42] The congressional careers of these men, who were considerably older than McKinley and Aldrich, included service during the Civil War period[43] and reflected a measure of disagreement with the ultra-protectionist creed. The concern felt by Allison and Sherman over signs of Western discontent with the postwar continuation of high tariff legislation coincided with Garfield's belief that indifference to the demands for tariff reform would result in violent and indiscriminate reduction.[44]

As early as 1870 Allison as a member of the Ways and Means Committee had departed from the majority view in regard to the question of protection. In so doing he advocated at least a twenty per cent decrease in duties on all leading articles and declared that insistence upon the retention of the high rates would result only in hastening the day of radical reduction.[45] Two years later Sherman in the same vein advised high tariff lobbyists that their interests would suffer less from permitting a slight decrease in rates than from inviting a struggle which would threaten the entire protectionist system.[46]

During the emotion-laden post-Civil War period when suggestions favoring tariff reduction resulted in charges of free trade sympathies and unpatriotic designs,[47] even such mild protests as those registered by Allison and Sherman may have indicated a degree of courage. Yet their admonitions proved ineffective. It should be noted, moreover, that despite their professed leanings toward moderation these two Republican statesmen chose, in accord with their concepts of party loyalty and regularity, to cast their votes and raise their voices in favor of the high tariff legislation to which they objected.[48]

Yet Sherman, despite his support of the act of 1883, took pains to point out what he regarded as its shortcomings, and to convey the impression that these were to be ascribed to the activities of other influential Senators. That law would have been satisfactory, he declared, if it had embodied the recommendations of the Tariff Commission.[49] Numerous defects, he maintained, had resulted from the failure to incorporate those suggestions.[50] Especially objectionable to him was the twenty per cent reduction on wool, a provision

adopted despite his "most strenuous efforts" to eliminate it from the measure.[51] The responsibility for
this unsatisfactory legislation, according to Sherman,
lay not with himself, but rather with other members
of the Finance and conference committees, especially
with Aldrich and Morrill.[52]

Following the enactment of the law of 1883, the
tariff continued to serve as a basis for controversy,
thus defying the alleged hope of Sherman and others
that the matter would cease to be a political issue and
would become "a purely business" question.[53] Aided
by the persistence of discord within the opposition
party regarding tariff reduction,[54] Republican orators
such as McKinley could conveniently keep themselves
in the public eye by castigating as unpatriotic and
calamitous the so-called "free trade" designs of
Democrats who advocated downward revision. It was
against the Morrison bill of 1884[55] that McKinley
again chose to make the most of "an opportunity to
display his wonderful command of the tariff subject,
to patriotically oppose the destruction of industrial
America."[56]

Yet despite their repeated and presumably patriotic
warnings against the menace of "free trade," Republican protectionists had little cause for disturbance
prior to the issuance of President Cleveland's stir-
ring tariff message in the final month of 1887. For
although his views regarding tariff reduction were
generally known, his action in according the question
his exclusive attention in his annual message of December 6, 1887[57] was regarded as a startling approach
to the problem.[58] A major consequence of this message, by which Cleveland made the tariff a definite
party issue,[59] was an unprecedented solidification of
the protectionist forces.[60]

In following a course indicated by Blaine, who

eagerly criticized the message and demonstrated his readiness to accept the tariff question as the leading issue in the approaching campaign,[61] Republicans could conspicuously denounce the Democratic President as the principal foe of the protective system. Cleveland's anti-protectionist address, McKinley charged, constituted an infuriated, wild, reckless, and illogical attack upon a policy productive of many blessings and supported by such great Americans as Washington, Jefferson, and Lincoln.[62] In McKinley's opinion and that of his partisan colleagues on the Ways and Means Committee, President Cleveland's views were incorporated in the proposed Democratic tariff measure known as the Mills bill. If approved, it would, according to these Republicans, "disturb every branch of business, retard manufacturing and agricultural prosperity, and seriously impair our industrial independence."[63]

Yet the Mills bill, against which McKinley chose to level such sweeping charges, neither called for any appreciable reduction[64] nor stood any chance of being passed by the Republican-controlled Senate. Indeed, a prolonged congressional deadlock over the tariff was anticipated by both parties. Involved in the strategy adopted by the Republicans was the consumption of much time in criticizing the Mills bill,[65] and the preparation by their majority in the upper chamber of a substitute for the House measure. Thus was the attempt successfully made to create a legislative stalemate which while preventing the enactment of either bill would provide opportunity for the delivery of protracted tariff speeches intended to be of use in the campaign of 1888.[66]

Generally regarded as representing opposing points of view in the campaign were the Democratic Mills bill and the Republican Senate substitute. This measure was viewed as the legislative embodiment of the high tariff stand incorporated in the party's platform of 1888, when the doctrine of protection assumed increased importance as a principle of Republican policy.[67] During the period of the prolonged tariff discussion indulged in by the House[68] prior to its passage of the Mills bill on July 21, 1888, many Republican protectionists directed their forensic energies to the reaffirmation of their high tariff faith. Among the members generally regarded as especially distinguishing themselves during the course of the extended debate were the fervent McKinley and his stout and towering colleague, Thomas B. Reed of Maine.[69]

In a speech before the House on May 18[70] McKinley so successfully recapitulated his high tariff arguments as to gain for himself, according to Olcott, national attention "as the ablest advocate of Protection in Congress."[71] McKinley granted that in some respects tariff legislation could be improved by revision. However, he again asserted that such a project, if undertaken at all, must be entrusted only to those who were friendly to the protective system. In the unwelcome approach of President Cleveland and the Democrats to the problem of revision, McKinley detected indications of unpatriotic statesmanship designed to promote antagonisms. In the high tariff program favored by Republicans, he professed to see, on the other hand, a system under which equal favors were accorded to all alike—manufacturers, farmers, laborers, tradesmen, consumers, and producers.

Objections to protection, McKinley declared, came not from enterprising citizens. The demand for the Democratic measure he attributed to the detrimental influences of alien importers, impractical college professors, and the independently wealthy. He referred to Democratic attacks upon the tariff as the mother of trusts as constituting the single novel feature introduced in the debates. McKinley assured his listeners that the tariff could not be held responsible for the trusts, which, he declared, originated in foreign nations addicted to free trade.

Yet despite this display of aptitude by McKinley in the familiar role of spokesman for protection during the "Great Debate," his performance was surpassed, according to Robinson, by that of Representative Reed.[72] Although less vocal than McKinley as an exponent of protection,[73] Reed, who had first been elected to the House in 1876, "was naturally a protectionist"[74] and as such provided aggressive representation for the textile manufacturers.[75] As a member of the Committee on Rules he had been highly instrumental in facilitating the passage of the tariff act of 1883. He had secured the timely adoption of a special rule which obviated the necessity of a two-thirds vote in order to bring the tariff legislation before the highly protectionist conference committee which gave the measure its final form.[76] In this manner he had brought the expiring lame duck Republican House to the effective support of Aldrich and his colleagues in the Senate.

It was in accord with Reed's high tariff sentiments as reflected in his earlier decisive service in behalf of protection that he addressed the House on May 19, 1888.[77] For nearly two hours he directed the full force of his commanding presence and forensic ability, sharpened by sarcasm and wit,[78] to the support of the protectionist doctrine. The Democrats Reed chided for violating, through their backing of the protectionist Mills bill, their own loudly professed tariff-for-revenue-only principles. The proposed measure, he pointed out, was subject to substantially the same criticisms as those hurled against the tariff legislation of 1883.

Reed denounced the Democratic argument that
tariff reduction would provide an expanding world
market for the products of this nation. In a flight of
isolationist rhetoric he utilized a fable by Aesop so
as to liken the foolish free trader to the befuddled
dog which in a mistaken attempt to improve its lot
sacrificed a choice shoulder of mutton. Like McKinley, Reed rose to the support of the protective system
as a positive good, so beneficial in its effects as to
be enjoyed by all sections, social classes, and economic groups. Also in accord with the views of Mc-
Kinley, Reed denied that the tariff was responsible
for the trusts, and he described as sheer raving the
criticism directed against them on that score.

Far from idle while their allies in the House supported the cause of protection were the Republicans
in the upper chamber. They had, since the introduction of the Mills bill, been at work on the preparation
of a counter proposal intended to be the protectionist
answer to the offensive Democratic measure.[79] Especially stirred by the inclusion in that bill of provisions
calling for reduced duties on iron and steel and cotton
and woolen goods was Senator Aldrich.[80] He took the
lead in the formulation of a measure which while putting his party on record for increased protection[81]
would satisfy even the extreme demands of such industrialists as James M. Swank, manager of the
American Iron and Steel Association.[82] Uninhibited
by any thought of moderation, Aldrich was not at all
favorably impressed by the retention of the protective
principle in the Mills bill or by the relatively high
duties provided by it. He thus saw no impropriety in
sponsoring and guiding through the Senate a measure
which bore the earmarks of having been framed almost exclusively in the interests of manufacturers.[83]

That Aldrich played the leading role in the formulation of the Republican answer to the Mills bill and in the strategy of focusing national attention upon the protectionist doctrine was indicated in a communication to him from Senator Morrill of Vermont.[84] "I fully comprehend the Herculean task of preparing this substitute," the aging and ailing nominal chairman of the Finance Committee wrote to its most powerful member.[85] Morrill also credited Senator Aldrich with "special honor" for his part in the preparation of the majority report. That document, which praised the Republican tariff policy and severely condemned that of the Democrats, Morrill described as containing "merciless logic" and as being instrumental in tearing the House measure "into pitiable fragments."[86]

The Senate substitute is often referred to as the "Allison bill" because of the Iowan's position at the head of the sub-committee to which the Mills bill was sent, and because it was he who reported the substitute to the Senate.[87] However, it would seem appropriate, in view of the much more active part played by the Rhode Island Senator, to apply to the measure the title which Morrill came to use, namely, the "Aldrich substitute."[88]

Outside Congress the great tariff controversy of 1888 was waged on the broader horizon of the national political campaign,[89] where agreeably voicing the praises of protection in the capacity of his party's standard bearer was Benjamin Harrison.[90] In his numerous stump speeches he left no doubts as to his orthodox Republicanism regarding the tariff question. And as if to avoid any suspicion that he was a recent convert to the protectionist doctrine, he averred that he had held to it since he had been "old enough to have opinions or to utter them."[91]

In keeping with the views of his partisan colleagues, presidential-candidate Harrison maintained that the benefits of protection were enjoyed by all[92] and that the system was vital for preserving the domestic market for Americans.[93] The Republicans, he stated, in his letter of acceptance, would "revise the schedule" and "modify rates, but always with an intelligent provision as to the effect upon domestic productions and the wages of our working people."[94]

In the Democratic threat of tariff reduction Harrison discerned not only the menace of industrial prostration,[95] but also the peril of special harm to the welfare of the laboring class.[96] For although he took pleasure in calling attention to the relatively prosperous condition of American workers,[97] he asserted that the lowering of wages would result from the decrease of duties.[98] And not only would wage reductions, in his view, accompany the Democratic attempt to provide lower prices through tariff decreases, but there was danger that the "cheapening process" would be "pushed so far as to involve the cheapening of human life and the loss of human happiness."[99]

The Mills bill Harrison regarded as a Democratic attempt to move the nation in the direction of "practical free trade."[100] His fear of such an eventuality he emphasized by expressing the belief that protection was "essential to the prosperity and possibly to the perpetuity of our Government."[101]

In a campaign during which such views formed the basis of protectionist appeals for votes, Harrison and his fellow Republicans gained for their party the power to control the executive and both legislative branches of the government. Yet whether the narrow victory by which this feat was accomplished should, despite Cleveland's plurality of 100,000 votes, be regarded as a mandate in favor of continuing high protection is a matter upon which there has been disagreement. According to Stanwood, "the tariff had been the only real issue in the canvass, and the Republicans had a right to treat the result as a popular verdict for protection, and as a commission to make a tariff law of their own."[102] Yet other authorities hold that in view of the plurality of popular votes cast for Cleveland, and because of the effects of vote purchasing in closely contested states, the election results cannot properly be regarded as a coherent expression of the electorate in favor of protection.[103]

Also the subject of some disagreement is the question as to whether there was a commitment on the part of the Republican protectionists to reduce import duties. Statements made by party leaders, including McKinley and Harrison, to the effect that Republicans were not averse to modification of the tariff if undertaken by its friends were widely interpreted as indicating that such revision would be in a downward direction. Such declarations, according to Dunn, were regarded by "almost everybody" as meaning that the tariff "would be reduced, but in such limited degree as to be still protective."[104] Noyes, on the other hand, although he recognizes that Republicans indicated they would decrease the rates, maintains that there was but slight basis for such expectations. In support of this contention he points to the party platform declarations and to a query by Morton as to whether revision in the interests of protection would not reflect greater wisdom and patriotism than would downward modification.[105]

Whatever the validity of the grounds for the expectation that the incoming Republicans would reduce the tariff, their leaders did not contemplate such action. Yet they were confronted by the disquieting problem as to how, in view of the slender margin by which they controlled Congress, they could enact legislation providing for increased protection.

So slight were the Republican congressional majorities gained in the election of 1888[106] as to give genuine cause for grave concern on the part of the administration. Disturbed, indeed, was Harrison over signs of party weakness patent in the slim Republican majorities and menacing to the prospects of the proposed protectionist legislation. In February, 1889 he expressed his fear in rejecting Blaine's suggestion for hasty action on the tariff by an extra session. Harrison believed that such an approach would constitute a precocious strain on the party, and that "with our narrow margin we may be successfully obstructed or may even divide over a tariff bill."[107]

This early expression of anxiety may be regarded as indicating Harrison's recognition of conflicting Republican views on the tariff question and his inclination to attach great importance to the role of the legislative department in the determination of policy. Harrison did not view the executive branch as a stronghold to be utilized in forcefully directing the course of congressional action. As President he perceived no necessity for guiding a governmental department which he regarded essentially in the light of a self-contained and self-propelled unit. Beyond the point of sedulous compliance with the traditional practice of addressing Congress through formal messages he felt no desire to go.[108]

To a man who possessed no outstanding traits of leadership, who was unusually reserved in manner, and who had served a term in the United States Senate,[109] such a negative view of the relation of the presidential office to Congress appeared both dignified and proper. In Harrison's predilection for a predominantly congressional type of government, under which Republican legislators would be very instrumental in the formulation of policy, were reflected elements of his personality and experience. In connection with his special regard for the upper chamber, we are informed by Dunn that Harrison was "deeply imbued with the importance of the Senate."[110]

Among the Republican Senators for whom Harrison expressed deep respect was John Sherman,[111] whose not altogether unsolicited advice included the remarks that "The President should 'touch elbows' with Congress. He should have no policy distinct from that of his party, and this is better represented in Congress than in the Executive."[112] In accord with this counsel Harrison proved quite willing to conduct himself in a retiring manner unobjectionable to politically ambitious legislators who sought ever greater honors for themselves.[113] And the pattern thus set would be in keeping with subsequent Republican rule in the period presently under consideration.

THE MCKINLEY TARIFF

That Harrison as President had lost none of the
faith in protection voiced by him during the campaign
he made clear in his inaugural address of March 4,
1889,[1] and in his first annual message to Congress on
December 3 of the same year.[2] Although in each of
these communications he referred to the troublesome
problem of the surplus, he regarded it as secondary
in importance to the tariff. He believed, he declared
in his inaugural remarks, that the necessary decrease
in revenue could be effected "without breaking down
our protective tariff or seriously injuring any domestic industry."[3] Harrison advocated the unimpaired retention of the protective system, and he expressed the
belief that no substantial yearly surplus need remain
following congressional expenditures for such purposes as debt resumption, liberalized pensions, and
ship construction. He thus indicated his agreement
with the dominant Republican view that neither the
surplus nor any considerations of economy should be
allowed to stand in the way of the contemplated high
tariff legislation.

In his first annual message President Harrison
again asserted that the maintenance of protection
should be regarded as more important than the danger
of surplus revenue. Attention, he declared, should
not be restricted to the surplus, but should be directed
toward "the just and reasonable protection of our
home industries."[4] He counseled "the wise and patriotic legislator" to broaden his outlook to embrace an
understanding of the relation of the tariff "to home

production, to work, to wages, and to the commercial
independence of our country."[5] At the same time
Harrison made what Noyes describes as "exceedingly
dangerous" recommendations for extravagant expenditures on increased pensions, river and harbor im-
provements, and coastal defenses.[6] And, in accord
with the view that the Republican victory in 1888 had
constituted a mandate for protectionist legislation, the
President called for a modification of the administra-
tive provisions and the schedules of the existing tariff
act.

Yet success in securing the approval of such legislation by the narrowly Republican House would require far more than Harrison's agreeable recommendations. Of primary necessity in freeing that chamber
from legislative paralysis and in permitting the passage of a tariff bill and of other party measures was
the imposition of procedural changes which would
eliminate filibustering tactics. These, under the long
period of Democratic control,[7] had been developed to
such a point that the legislative process could be
seriously impeded by a single determined obstructionist Representative,[8] and brought to a standstill by
a substantial minority.[9]

Under hitherto accepted procedure, legislative action could be prevented through indulgence in such
practices as the refusal to answer roll calls and the
making of dilatory motions. Thus there existed little
likelihood of securing House approval of legislation
even when the margin of the majority party happened
to be large. And so slim was the Republican advantage in the fifty-first Congress that even in the ab-
sence of filibustering, the requirement that a quorum
must be determined by the calling of the roll would
have permitted the enactment of only such legislation
as might secure Democratic approval. For, as the

Democrats would remain silent during roll calls, the Republicans would find it impossible to assemble the 165 Representatives required for a quorum under the existing practice. Thus any transaction of business by the House would probably have been limited to such formal matters as would have had the approval of both parties.[10]

From such a plight, however, the Republicans were rescued through Speaker Reed's insistence upon exercising his power in a manner daringly calculated to insure majority rule while bringing his colleagues to the support of party policy. In harmony with the view expressed by Sherman and accepted by Harrison, Reed believed that the best interests of the Republicans called for "a preponderance of power in Congress, and not in the White House."[11] As "one of the very few Americans who gained eminence in public life entirely on the basis of service in the House of Representatives,"[12] he had long been interested in bringing that chamber to the effective support of his party. Yet earlier in his congressional career, when the Republicans constituted the minority, he had supported the very obstructionist tactics[13] which when later regarded as a barrier to the implementation of the party's program he determined to eliminate.[14]

Possessed of a background of legislative experience which included membership on the Judiciary, Ways and Means, and Rules Committees, Reed was well qualified for the speakership. From the time of his appointment to the Judiciary Committee in the forty-sixth Congress he had manifested great interest in matters of House procedure. His knowledge of the organization of the lower chamber evoked from Henry Cabot Lodge the declaration that Reed "not only knew thoroughly the complicated rules of the House, but, what is even rarer, he was equally master of general

parliamentary law and understood, as very few men
do, the theory and philosophy of the system."[15]

In keeping with Reed's growing reputation as a
parliamentarian had been his rising prominence as
marked by his already noted contribution as a member of the Rules Committee in clearing the way for
the enactment of the tariff legislation of 1883.[16] Partisan recognition of his parliamentary skill had
brought to him in 1885 the Republican nomination for
the speakership, an honor which during periods of
Democratic majorities placed him in the position of
minority floor leader.[17]

Following his election to the speakership,[18] Reed
boldly sought to secure House adoption of the rules
necessary to give effective control to the majority
party. In this undertaking he was motivated by the
belief that the election of 1888 had constituted a general mandate for legislation.[19] Moreover, he was
probably aware of what Robinson refers to as the
"decidedly unpleasant element of truth" in the Democratic charges that the Republicans were obligated to
enact tariff legislation beneficial to those who had
made campaign contributions.[20] Reflected in Reed's
fearless conduct were careful planning and his willingness to resign from Congress in case he should
fail in his objective.[21] Rather than to risk the defeat
of his project by opening the way for prolonged debate
through the adoption by the Republicans of rules
authorizing the counting of a quorum, he resorted to
a radical application of his power as Speaker.[22]

In an unprecedented ruling which highlighted his
success in reorganizing the House, Reed held, on
January 29, 1890, that the determination of a quorum
was henceforth to be based upon the actual presence
rather than upon the officially self-acknowledged
presence of members.[23] Involved in his method of

effecting reform in the legislative process was a revolutionary assumption of authority[24] which no amount of explanation would be able to conceal.[25] Despite a three-day period of bedlam arising from Democratic opposition to a ruling assailed as the dictatorial decision of a usurper and a czar,[26] Reed's decision stood. Successful in maintaining a high degree of composure, the Speaker, after being sustained, on appeal, by a majority of the quorum, refused thenceforth to entertain appeals from his drastic ruling on the basis that the House had already settled that point.[27]

With the solid support of his party[28] Speaker Reed was able not only to frustrate further Democratic attempts at obstruction[29] but was likewise successful in consolidating his gains by securing the adoption on February 14 of a revised code. Primarily his own creation, this work, which provided for comprehensive reforms intended to vest in the majority party effective control of the House, bore the fitting appellation, "Reed Rules."[30]

For the purpose of ending obstruction the "Reed rules" included four revolutionary provisions. These clothed the speaker with power to refuse motions which he regarded as dilatory, specified that quorums be determined on the basis of attendance, reduced the Committee of the Whole and simplified its procedure, and revised the order of House business. Through the revised code, which "unquestionably meant a great increase in the power of the Speaker,"[31] Reed was enabled to secure productive action on the tariff and other features of his party's program. He thus rendered largely meaningless, as far as the House was concerned, such anxieties as those earlier expressed by Harrison regarding the dangers involved in the slender Republican numerical advantage. By

the application of careful forethought, unexcelled au-
dacity, and commendable composure, Reed brought
despotic powers to the aid of his party[32] and thus became an indispensable leader in promoting its policy.

To the extent that he felt the need, Reed, in dominating the House in the interest of the Republican
party, utilized the services of his chief competitor
for the speakership, Representative McKinley. He
was assigned to the chairmanship of the Ways and
Means Committee, a position whose responsibilities
included sponsorship of fiscal measures and leadership on the floor.[33] This recognition of McKinley, for
whom Reed had no great admiration,[34] in no way de-
tracted from the autocratic power of the Speaker, who,
as chairman of the Committee on Rules regarded his
Republican subordinates in that body as mere
lieutenants.[35]

Nevertheless, the appointment of McKinley to the
chairmanship of the Ways and Means Committee
proved highly beneficial to his career. In that position he had charge of the initiation of legislation on
the tariff, then regarded as the major political issue
before the nation. Thus, by virtue of the assignment,
McKinley could reap publicity on a hitherto unattain-
able scale. The resulting amplification of his image
as a high tariff advocate would contribute, in combination with the decisive support accorded him by his
good friend, Mark Hanna, to the elevation of McKinley
to the presidency, despite competitive activity on the
part of Reed.[36]

For even if full agreement be accorded Robinson's
claim that the rehabilitation of the Republican party
was attributable in greater measure to Speaker Reed
"than to any other leader,"[37] his contribution in this
regard did not make him a widely liked individual.
Much less popular than McKinley,[38] Reed suffered not

only from his representation of a state which was not
politically strategic, but also from negative public reaction to his peremptory rule of the House. In spite
of initial public approval of his reformative feat, the
dictatorial methods which he used in converting that
chamber into an efficient party instrument came to be
viewed as inexcusably oppressive.[39] So marked was
the negative effect of his high-handed action as to
render futile his subsequently observed efforts to exercise caution in his management of the House in
order to avoid impairing his chances for the
presidency.[40]

Yet if Reed's autocratic conduct in the speakership
weakened his presidential prospects, those of McKinley were probably strengthened by the imposition of
strict controls in the lower chamber. In addition to
gaining a vantage point for publicity through his appointment by Reed to the head of the Ways and Means
Committee, the tactful Ohioan was enabled, as a result of the reorganization of the House, to give a good
account of himself as the Republican floor leader.
According to Robinson, McKinley was "on the whole,
a successful leader on the floor, although it is hard
to tell how much of his success in this capacity was
due to the rigorous party discipline enforced by the
Speaker."[41]

Little time was lost by McKinley in directing his
energies to the formulation of a tariff measure destined to make him "in the eyes of the country more
than ever the most conspicuous exponent of the theory
and practice of high protection."[42] In the promotion
of the "New Protectionism,"[43] a pro-industrialist
movement which sought through the authorization of
excessively high duties to reduce the surplus and
bring allegedly unlimited benefits to the nation, he
served in the vanguard of his party. By Olcott, Mc-

Kinley is praised as possessing "the dominating mind" of the committee charged with preparing the tariff measure, and as impressing upon the bill "the unmistakable imprint of his own positive ideas of protective principles."[44]

Not to be overlooked, however, is the fact that as the basis of the bill of 1890 McKinley used the Senate substitute of 1888,[45] largely the work of Aldrich. Nor is it certain that in the preparation of the House measure McKinley limited that solon's influence to the utilization of his bill as the foundation of the new measure. For the inclusion in the House bill of Aldrich's policy of extending greater favors to the refiners than to the growers of sugar is recognized by Stephenson as a possible indication of the acceptance of advice offered by the powerful Senator from Rhode Island.[46]

In the probable hope of escaping such criticisms as had been directed against the Democratic formulation of the so-called "dark lantern" Mills bill,[47] chairman McKinley utilized an approach which allotted almost four months to hearings, beginning immediately following the December, 1889 holidays.[48] Only two weeks were allowed for the actual discussion of the bill in the Reed-ruled lower chamber.[49] Tariff hearings, according to Tarbell, "perhaps were never less justifiable," in view of the fact that they could succeed only in duplicating the great amount of recently recorded testimony already available for the edification of the Ways and Means Committee. The devoutly protectionist McKinley, however, had not the slightest intention of dispensing with such traditional ceremony.[50]

As if sensitive to Democratic charges that labor, unlike manufacturers, did not enjoy the privilege of being heard by the committee,[51] McKinley asserted

that hearings were open to all interested groups.
These included "manufacturers, merchants, farmers,
Grangers, members of the Farmers' Alliance, agents,
factors, wool-growers,—freetraders and protectionists."[52] Though the demands of industrialists who had
made liberal campaign contributions may have been
disagreeable to less ardent protectionists than Mc-
Kinley, he gave sympathetic attention "to any one
representing a worthy interest that seemed to need an
increased duty."[53]

Indicative of the abiding nature of McKinley's protectionist faith were the pronouncements contained in
the April 16 majority report of the Ways and Means
Committee,[54] and in his May 7 speech to the House.
In the majority report of the proposed measure, which
was styled "A bill to reduce the revenue and equalize
the duty on imports, and for other purposes," Mc-
Kinley and his colleagues gave re-assurance of the
persistence of their high tariff ardor. What they
chose to regard as their equitable approach to tariff
revision had not been undertaken, the report declared,
in a manner calculated to restrict their vision to the
mere matter of revenue reduction.

To the preservation of the protective system, the
majority report stated, careful attention had been
given by the Ways and Means Committee. It had
framed the measure with the view of promoting the
welfare of all Americans, and of benefiting the producing and laboring classes. The committee had
without hesitation, according to the report, made increases in duties whenever necessary to provide protection to the extent of differences between domestic
and foreign production costs in order to prevent
detrimental effects upon American manufacturing or
labor. The bill should be passed, McKinley and his
committee supporters recommended, not only to pro-

mote existing industries but to initiate new ones as
well. And the report made much of the presumed advantages to be enjoyed by agriculture through the inclusion in the proposed measure of increased duties
on farm products.[55]

In language more glowing than that employed in the
majority report, McKinley on May 7 repeated the
tenets of the high tariff doctrine in the initial address
of the brief House debate on the pending measure.[56]
To the protective system he attributed the country's
unusual strides "in arts, in science, in literature, in
manufacture, in wealth and credit, and National
honor." The retention and progressive development
of that system he regarded as having been definitely
demanded in the electoral contest of 1888. That campaign he viewed as having been waged on the tariff
issue to the practical exclusion of all other matters.

"If any one thing was settled by the election of
1888," McKinley asserted in his May 7 address, "it
was that the protective policy, as promulgated in the
Republican platform and heretofore inaugurated and
maintained by the Republican party, should be secured
in any fiscal legislation to be had by the Congress
chosen in that great contest and upon that mastering
issue." The voters had spoken and he was glad to
interpret the outcome of their balloting as a demand
for tariff revision based upon "full recognition of the
principle and purpose of protection." Thus, McKinley
assured his hearers, the measure under consideration represented the committee's compliance with the
popular will.[57]

"Experience has demonstrated," McKinley further
declared in his May 7 speech, "that for us and ours,
and for the present and the future, the protective system meets our wants, our conditions, promotes the
National design, and will work out our destiny better

than any other." In what he referred to as the pre-
Civil War Democratic "revenue tariff" he found the
cause of the depressed condition of the economy in
1860. In the Republican and "thoroughly American"
protective tariff,[58] on the other hand, McKinley detected the driving force of progress. This impetus
was, in his view, reflected in industrial expansion
and in a prosperity so abounding as to provide the
nation with well-nigh incomprehensible wealth and
the workingmen with "splendid deposits in savings
banks."

American achievements in manufacturing, in mining, and in agriculture McKinley regarded as the result of a tariff system which promoted free-enterprise
economy by stimulating inventive aptitude and permitting generous remuneration for the work of men's
minds and hands. The "country's highest development
and greatest prosperity," he maintained, could be
attained only by means of protectionist legislation.[59]
From protection, McKinley believed, were to be de-
rived "the greatest gains to the people, the greatest
comforts to the masses, the widest encouragement
for manly aspirations, with the largest rewards, dig-
nifying and elevating our citizenship, upon which the
safety and purity and permanency of our political
system depend."

In the provisions of the tariff bill purportedly designed to assure such benefits as these was mirrored
McKinley's preoccupation with meeting the extremist
demands of manufacturers rather than with promoting
the welfare of farmers and consumers. Motivated by
the desire to foster domestic industries, McKinley,
who favored the imposition of prohibitive rates[60] while
resisting any method of revenue reduction regarded
as inimical to the interests of manufacturers, supported the removal of the raw sugar duty and opposed
the Blaine-inspired drive for reciprocity.

Obviously in harmony with the principle of benefiting domestic industrialists by permitting the monopolistic sugar trust to secure raw sugar at decreased prices[61] and thus paving the way for additional millions in profits to the sugar refiners,[62] was the removal of the duty from raw sugar. Yet this feature of the tariff legislation was represented by McKinley as a great boon to the consumers.[63] In the view of staunch protectionists there was no reason why an arrangement aimed at drastically reducing the revenue[64] in a manner so profitable to the sugar trust should not at the same time be portrayed as especially beneficial to the consuming public. The McKinleyites, moreover, regarded the remission of the raw sugar duty as a means of mitigating agrarian discontent. This provision, they contended, would be helpful in counteracting Western dissatisfaction with increased rates on manufactured products and in offsetting unwelcome accusations that the Republican tariff measure was heavily weighted in favor of the wealthy classes.[65]

McKinley, in line with his determination to subordinate the considerations of foreign commerce to the interests of domestic industries, turned a deaf ear in 1890 to proposals pointing the way toward reciprocity.[66] Apparent in his attitude was the fear of the ultra-protectionists that the concept of reciprocal commercial concessions constituted an opening free trade wedge menacing to the high tariff system.[67] He succeeded in gaining House approval of his bill in a form untainted by such apostasy as that urged by the ardent advocate of reciprocity, Secretary of State Blaine.[68]

In his enthusiasm over his project of fostering greater Pan-American accord,[69] Blaine sought through the incorporation of reciprocity provisions to make the tariff measure more palatable to the West and of greater service to his party and perhaps also to his persisting presidential aspirations.[70] He disagreed with McKinley's view that the election of 1888 had constituted a demand for higher duties.[71] It was Blaine's professed belief that the welfare of the party depended upon providing the Western farmer with a market in Latin America. As early as February 10, prior to the completion of the measure by the Ways and Means Committee, he had begun his dramatic if rather disappointing reciprocity struggle. On that date he had unsuccessfully attempted to persuade the Republicans on the committee to retain the raw sugar duty as a bargaining advantage in securing reciprocal trade concessions.[72]

Intended to soothe the same Western farmers whose favor was sought in connection with the removal of the raw sugar duty and Blaine's reciprocity proposal was the inclusion in the tariff bill of what Stanwood refers to as "a complete schedule of protective duties upon products of agriculture."[73] These provisions, regarded by Rhodes as a manifestation of "clever politics" on the part of the protectionist Republicans,[74] were highlighted by rate increases on such articles as meats, grains, butter, and potatoes, and by the addition of eggs to the dutiable list. This section of the measure was ridiculed by the opposition as an absurd pretense of alarm over foreign competition, in view of this nation's foremost rank in exporting grains and other food products.[75]

Yet the advocates of protection exploited the agricultural provisions in decreasing Western resistance to high tariffs by instilling in credulous farmers the feeling that they too had come to be included in the protective system. Stanwood concedes the general ineffectiveness, from an economic standpoint, of this

phase of the legislation. He observes, however, that
the farmers "could no longer complain that they were
left at the mercy of circumstances when the manufacturers were favored," and that as a result of the
attention accorded the agrarians they joined their
fellow Republicans of the East in the support of
protection.[76]

Much nearer McKinley's heart than the incorporation in the tariff bill of the psychologically and politically effective agricultural provisions was his success
in raising the duty on tin plate to 2.2 cents per pound
as compared with the single cent allowed by the act of
1883.[77] This provision was regarded by high tariff
enthusiasts as the "most enlightened" phase of the
McKinley bill.[78] The increased duty was directed, in
line with "a policy of fostering the embryo, rather
than of protecting the infant,"[79] toward avoiding the
repetition of earlier unsuccessful attempts at the inclusion of the tin plate industry. This objective, from
the standpoint of zealous protectionists, seemed
"entirely reasonable and justifiable."[80]

As the embodiment of high tariff aspirations the
McKinley bill secured House approval[81] as the result
of a concerted effort in which the chairman of the
Ways and Means Committee and the Speaker effectively joined hands. Involved in this protectionist
achievement was Reed's co-operation in a McKinley-
maneuvered compromise. This committed the party,
in return for the support of the tariff measure by
pro-silver Republicans, to concessions looking toward
the subsequent enactment of silver purchase legislation.[82] For the Speaker's role in jamming through a
measure which both he and McKinley later admitted
included excessively high duties[83] Reed was subjected
to considerable criticism, some of which emanated
from Republicans.[84]

Following the hurried passage of the tariff bill by what Reed himself described as the non-deliberative House,[85] he exhibited marked impatience over the comparatively slow progress of the measure in a Senate which at times became the object of his contemptuous remarks.[86] The delay of the McKinley bill in that chamber, preventing presidential approval until October 1, reflected the conflicting interests which necessitated concessions to the Senate silverites, to the Southern members, and to the Blaine-inspired exponents of reciprocity. In the arrangement of truces directed at reconciling Republican differences to the extent required for the enactment of the priority-rated tariff measure, a leading role appears to have been played by Reed's "close friend," Senator Aldrich.[87]

In effecting a compromise calculated to parry Blaine's telling blows for reciprocity during the consideration of the tariff bill in the Senate,[88] Aldrich executed "a strategic retreat."[89] In the course of this maneuver he substituted a negative form of reciprocity for the positive type sought by Blaine and also managed to secure considerable publicity through the application of the title, "Aldrich amendment," to the long delayed provision. To this strategy the Rhode Island Senator resorted only after an indication of the futility of the protectionist effort to minimize the effect of Blaine's pleas by castigating reciprocity as a disguised form of free trade. And despite Aldrich's lack of real appreciation for the importance of the West,[90] he would appear to have been sufficiently aware of that section's dissatisfaction over silver,[91] and of the favorable Western reception accorded Blaine's proposal for expanding markets,[92] to recognize the expediency of a limited degree of compromise.

The negative reciprocity amendment introduced by Aldrich on August 28[93] did not conform with the end sought by Blaine.[94] Aldrich's proposal was based upon the confidential advice of his friend, President Harrison. Sugar, he had suggested, could well be left on the free list, despite Blaine's objection, and the Chief Executive could be empowered to re-impose duties on that commodity if nations exporting it to this country should fail to reciprocate by the extension of equivalent benefits.[95]

Implicit in this arrangement was a limitation of the range of effective promotional activity that could be undertaken by Blaine. By leaving sugar duty-free the Aldrich amendment, as reported and passed, deprived the Secretary of the positive bargaining advantage which could have been made available by the adoption of Blaine's suggestion for the retention of the sugar duty. Under the Aldrich proposal the executive department was given only the negative and contingent power of imposing specified punitive assessments against nations regarded as failing to grant equivalent reciprocal advantages for the free admission into this country of sugar, tea, coffee, molasses, and hides.[96]

Regarded as less objectionable than the Blaine proposal[97] by ultra-protectionists and Senators opposed to expansion of executive authority, Aldrich's amendment demonstrated his ability to promote the high tariff cause while preventing the increase of executive power. In the adoption of the Aldrich amendment rather than the Blaine proposal, the upper chamber "held its ground, unwilling to accord an unwonted treaty-making and economic bargaining power to the President."[98] Aldrich, in securing the incorporation of his own amendment in the tariff measure of 1890, reduced to the category of a mere gesture the re-

ciprocity legislation sought by Blaine.[99] Following
the adoption of the reciprocity amendment by the Senate on September 10,[100] Aldrich served on a conference committee whose membership included Sherman,
Allison, McKinley, and Dingley. The report of this
committee was approved by the House on September
27 and by the upper branch three days later.[101]

Emphasized by Aldrich's adroitness in securing
the ratification of his reciprocity amendment was his
influential role in determining the character of the
tariff act of 1890, a service for which he received reiterated recognition from chairman Morrill.[102] By
Stanwood, Aldrich is credited as being responsible
for "the adjustment and harmonization of duties and
the character of the completed measure."[103] So effective indeed were his efforts that the legislation as
enacted constituted "a complete victory" on the part
of men bent upon saddling the nation with tariffs so
high as to leave no doubt of the Republican party's
repudiation of earlier pledges looking toward downward revision.[104]

For this protectionist triumph and for Aldrich's
contributions, approbation was forthcoming from high
tariff exponents in and out of Congress. The measure, in McKinley's view, despite the inclusion of the
reciprocity provision, "was protective in every para-
graph, and American in every line and word."[105]
Among the expressions of appreciation were those of
industrialists who showered great praise upon Aldrich
for his highly effective advocacy of their cause in the
Senate.[106]

By such organizations as the Iron and Steel Association, the Industrial League, and the National Association of Wool Manufacturers, he was regarded as
the fulfillment of their desire for a really skillful,
energetic, and technically informed legislator who

would accept industrialist dictation in the preparation
of tariff schedules.[107] Characterized by Tarbell as
"the first entirely able and . . . entirely cynical
leader" developed by the exponents of high protection,[108] Aldrich was publicly acclaimed by the National
Association of Wool Manufacturers. In a bulletin issued by that organization he was commended for his
services in managing the tariff measure. He was
described as being remarkably well versed regarding
complicated schedules, and as being ever watchful
and disinclined to talk unless indulgence in such activity was necessary.[109]

Recognized by industrialists as the outstanding
leader of the protectionist cause, Aldrich has been
variously referred to as "the leader of the United
States Senate,"[110] "the general manager of the United
States,"[111] "the boss of the United States,"[112] and as
"Morgan's floor broker."[113] Through his work in the
formulation and enactment of a measure designed for
the benefit of manufacturers, the Rhode Island Senator had done much to determine Republican policy.

Secure in the retention of his Senate seat because
of his representation of an industrial state of stable
political tendencies,[114] Aldrich had long been convinced of the propriety of industrialist pressure in
the sphere of legislation.[115] He held to the "matter of
course" view that for the tariff favors bestowed upon
manufacturers "he and his party should receive in
exchange what financial and organizing aid they required."[116] Apparently unimpressed by considerations
which led such colleagues as McKinley and Harrison
to portray protection as about equally beneficial to
all, Aldrich frankly admitted that the act of 1890 contemplated greater advantages for manufacturers than
for farmers or consumers.[117]

Indeed, with the passage of that legislation the Re-

publicans had given hitherto unequaled legislative
expression to the view that the national interest required little more than supplying the manufacturers
with a profusion of protectionist favors. In the enactment of this unprecedentedly high tariff measure,[118]
consideration had apparently been given only to producers while consumers were ignored.[119] And although some consumers may have taken comfort from
assurances that the average level of rates had been
increased only about four or five per cent,[120] the mere
quotation of an average rate could hardly be regarded
as accurately reflecting the actual protectionist gains
effected. Embodied in the law were hidden increases.
These resulted from broadening the application of
specific duties, which often overlapped ad valorem
duties, from imposing increased rates upon cheaper
grades of goods, and from restricting rate decreases
almost entirely to noncompetitive goods.[121]

Unhampered by considerations of raising additional
funds, the Republicans in 1890 gave life to the first
tariff measure avowedly dedicated primarily to the
cause of protection and only incidentally to the matter of revenue.[122] The troublesome problem of the
surplus, their leaders were determined, must not be
allowed to interfere with the major goal of securing
increased protection for industry. In line with this
resolution they had agreed that in addition to the imposition of prohibitive duties, the removal of raw
sugar duties, and the payment of the domestic sugar
bounty, there should be a reduction in the internal
taxes on alcohol and tobacco.[123]

Yet by a public faced with an immediate price rise
which was unaccompanied by any perceptible wage increase,[124] neither the reduction of internal taxes nor
the postponed removal of the raw sugar duty[125] was
regarded as sufficiently significant to warrant ap-

proval of the McKinley act as a whole. In demonstration of their dissatisfaction, the voters in the congressional elections of 1890, generally regarded as
a virtual referendum on the tariff act,[126] registered
their resentment against the law. In decisive fashion
they eliminated the narrow Republican advantage in
the House and installed a Democratic majority num-
bering 235 members as compared with 88 for the
party of protection.[127]

As a result of the widespread reaction against his
legislative namesake, McKinley was defeated in his
attempt to secure an eighth consecutive term in the
lower chamber.[128] The Democratic victory he chose
to regard as the outcome of an effective conspiracy
composed of importers and free traders for the purpose of creating increased prices to be ascribed to
the tariff act.[129] Yet Reed, more realistically, expressed the view that the McKinley act, by evoking
warnings and fears of rising costs, constituted the
major factor in the Republican setback.[130]

Although successful in meeting the high tariff demands of industrialists, the protectionist services of
Aldrich together with the indispensable work of Reed
and the contributions of McKinley figured heavily in
the removal of the Republicans from political ascen-
dancy. Reduced by the election of 1890 to what
Stephenson describes as "the futile party," their administration had from a legislative standpoint come
to an early end.[131]

So persistently obnoxious to the public did the
price increases resulting from the passage of the Mc-
Kinley act prove as to figure significantly in the re-
verses of the Republicans in the election of 1892. In
that contest they not only lost their hold on the presidency and their narrow advantage in the Senate, but
they again failed to gain control of the House. For

under the operation of a tariff whose dutiable list included such widely used items as food, clothing, carpets, blankets, agricultural implements, and cooking utensils, the flame of popular discontent did not subside. Resentment over the rising costs of flour, corn-meal, potatoes, and meat was further aggravated by price advances on lumber and coal, and especially by the increased charges for tin articles and canned products.[132]

In the electoral contest of 1892, according to Senator Cullom, "the question in general was the McKinley Law and its results." In the course of a campaign "entirely fought out on the tariff issue" the opposition party was "able to show that there had been increase in cost in many articles" viewed as necessities.[133] Thus aided, the Democrats managed to gain a victory in both branches of Congress and in the White House, a feat not previously accomplished during the postwar period.[134]

REPUBLICAN OPPOSITION TO DEMOCRATIC
TARIFF REFORM EFFORT

Apparently pleased to engage in controversy with the Democratic administration whose basic objectives so closely resembled their own,[1] the Republicans magnified their differences with the majority party in regard to the tariff, a question on which there was greater minority harmony than on the subject of silver. Although such Republican regulars as Senators Sherman and Cullom were well aware of the increasingly moderate trend of President Cleveland's tariff views,[2] they nevertheless joined in the charge that the depressed state of the economy had resulted from the tariff reform intentions of the Democratic party.[3] The Republican leaders, far from willing to recognize the necessity for tariff legislation,[4] indulged in their traditional practice of labeling the Democrats as the party of free trade.[5]

Apparent in the emphasis placed by the Republicans upon the allegedly harmful Democratic tariff policy was the determination to capitalize upon the issue of protection in their effort to regain control of the government in the elections of 1894 and 1896. Conducive to the realization of this objective was the relatively strong Republican position resulting to a large extent from the debilitating discord which permeated the ranks of the badly broken Democratic party.[6]

In directing their attack against their opponents, the Republicans found fault with the Democratic tariff bill whose preparation had been begun during the extra session.[7] Subjected to special condemnation were

the alleged refusal of the Ways and Means Committee
to provide adequate opportunity for the presentation
of protectionist views, and the utilization by that committee of assistance from the Treasury Department.[8]

Nor did the Democratic tariff measure, which
secured House approval on February 1, 1894,[9] and
which was a disappointment for many Democrats, including Representative Wilson,[10] escape Republican
condemnation as constituting free trade legislation.
Yet the inaccuracy of the charge would seem clear
from Taussig's observation that the reductions provided in the Wilson bill were "not enough, indeed, to
make it a revolutionary measure."[11] According to
Peck, the House-approved Democratic proposal not
only fell far short of providing for free trade but
"dealt considerately with the many interests" long
sheltered under the arm of Republican protectionism.[12]

Despite the generally conservative nature of the
Wilson bill,[13] the measure was resented by the Republicans. They objected to its deference to the
Democratic principle calling for the free admission
of the basic raw materials used in industry,[14] and
also to its inclusion of a two per cent tax upon incomes in excess of $4,000.[15] This provision, although
described by one authority as "extremely mild,"[16] was
backed by what the conservative opposition regarded
as "radical sentiment."[17]

Indicative of the accuracy of Cullom's explanation
that the policy of his party included opposition to a
tax on incomes[18] was the fact that of 182 House votes
cast in favor of the amendment, the Republicans fur-
nished only five.[19] If credibility is to be accorded in-
formation given out by Representative McMillan many
years after the House adoption of the income tax provision, this action would appear to have been made
possible through the connivance of Reed. Possibly in

the belief that harm would come to the party sponsoring such radical legislation, Reed allegedly exerted
his influence as a member of the Ways and Means
Committee to secure, despite Democratic opposition,
the quorum necessary for inserting the income tax
provisions in the Wilson bill.[20] Whatever the degree
of reliability properly ascribable to this allegation,
there is no doubt that on the day the Wilson bill passed
the House Reed openly attacked the measure in the
closing speech on the Republican side.[21]

In the course of this address Reed sought again to
convince others of the soundness of his own faith in
the blessings of the protective system, reiterating in
its defense stock Republican arguments. He regarded
the Wilson bill as unsatisfactory to both parties because of its failure to go far enough either in the direction of Republican protectionism or Democratic
free trade. If enacted, the measure would, in Reed's
opinion, serve only to aggravate the already preva-
lent depression and uncertainty. The bill's failure to
provide adequate protection would impede the operation of a system which had developed an extremely
high level of national welfare characterized by a
progressive civilization productive of great oppor-
tunities and possessed of unlimited potential.

Through the encouragement of high wages and of
invention, Reed held in his speech of February 1,
1894, protection had improved the condition of the
whole of American society. Yet the maintenance and
improvement of the wage scale, stressed by him as
an important objective, would be impossible under
the Wilson bill. For this measure, which in his view
was based on the erroneous Democratic idea that a
cleavage existed between producing and consuming
classes, constituted a proposal to reduce wages and
thus shrink the market. The high tariff system must

be maintained to assure for the future an ever increasing share of the prosperity which had been experienced under Republican protectionist legislation in the past.

Although Reed's words and the refusal of his party to support the Wilson bill did not prevent its passage in the House, Republican resistance was destined to meet with greater success in the Senate. In that chamber five months would elapse prior to the enactment of a heavily amended tariff measure on July 3. Highlighted by the lengthy struggle which exposed President Cleveland's failure as a party leader was the effectiveness with which the Republican minority, guided mainly by Aldrich, subjected the bill to a protectionist revision resulting in many rate increases ranging up to 300 per cent.[22] Among the circumstances contributing to this Republican accomplishment were the control of the Senate "by powerful financial interests,"[23] the narrow Democratic majority, the tradition of crossing party lines,[24] and Cleveland's decided unpopularity in the upper chamber.[25]

In turning to the fullest possible protectionist advantage a situation so promising, Aldrich gladly accepted the co-operation of a handful of insurgent Democrats headed by Senator Gorman of Maryland, a fellow advocate of the interests of the wealthy classes.[26] So vital was his service to the high tariff cause that the term "Gormanized"[27] has been applied to the process by which the moderate Wilson bill was transformed into the highly protectionist measure destined for enactment in the identical form approved by the Senate. Aided by the Gorman bloc, Aldrich, in a remarkable demonstration of insight and facility, effectively directed the energies of the minority Republicans to the perpetuation of the protective system.

Highly favorable to the attainment of the protectionist objective of the Republican minority was its possession of 38 seats in an upper chamber which contained only 44 Democrats and 4 Populists. Under this arrangement the defection of but 5 Democrats would be sufficient to defeat the Wilson bill or to require its revision along lines acceptable to the exponents of protection.[28] As more than that number of Democratic Senators felt that their local interests demanded protection not granted by the House-approved measure, Gorman succeeded in mustering an opposition bloc of Democrats sufficiently strong to guarantee increases in duties.[29]

From the time when the Wilson bill was sent to the Senate until early in May when the administration supporters yielded to the powerful protectionist opposition consisting of a combination of the Aldrich-led Republicans and the Democratic insurgents, progress in re-shaping the measure was largely undercover. Apprised in caucus that the bill would be defeated unless drastically revised in accord with the protectionist bias of the Gorman bloc, the administration Senators felt constrained to modify their conceptions as to what could be accomplished in the way of tariff reform.[30] After a delay of nearly two months, during which period amendments were added with the hope of securing protectionist approval, the measure as reported by the Finance Committee on March 20 still failed to overcome the objections of the insurgents.

At this juncture Senator Jones of Arkansas spent many days in consultation with discontented colleagues and agreed to the inclusion of some 400 additional amendments intended to clear the path for the passage of the bill. By Aldrich, who fully appreciated the magnitude of the revision being effected through numerous off-stage conferences, the Democratic tactics were followed with great acumen. This he indi-

cated in his reference on May 12 to an alleged understanding among the Senate Democrats that the measure was to go into operation in the form approved by
the upper branch, without submission to a group of
conferees representing both chambers.[31]

Although Aldrich would have preferred to keep the
McKinley act in operation,[32] he appeared to be reasonably satisfied with the headway made by the protectionist forces in the reconstruction of the House-
approved bill. Such was his satisfaction with the tariff
outlook that by mid-May "He slackened his pressure
upon the Democrats" and "began to allow things to
take their course," apparently confident that the majority party would extend due recognition to the protectionist principle.[33] Continual behind-the-scenes
negotiations, many of which were bipartisan, and a
Republican caucus which served as a preface to confidential discussions among Senate members had
rendered transitory the major obstacles confronting
the advocates of high tariffs.[34]

In the successful direction of his energies toward
the upward revision of the Democratic tariff bill,
Aldrich utilized the tactics of delay. The measure
would, he served notice, be held back until it was so
modified as to be acceptable to protectionists.[35] In
keeping with this intention he turned to protectionist
advantage the time-consuming investigation of alleged
sugar stock speculation by Senators during the preparation of the sugar schedule.[36] By opposing an attempt
to table the resolution calling for that investigation,
Aldrich indicated his desire to prevent the upper
chamber from giving its attention to the passage of
the tariff measure.[37]

From his Republican colleague, Senator Quay, who
openly acknowledged the sugar speculation charges,
Aldrich received telling support in the shape of out-

right filibustering. Unless the protectionists were
granted concessions in keeping with their demands,
Quay declared, the administration would get no tariff
legislation whatever. By indulgence in interminable
talk, he threatened, he would prevent approval of the
pending bill. The length to which he was prepared to
go in giving substance to his warning he demonstrated
by the persistence with which he applied himself to
an intermittent filibuster beginning on April 14 and
ending more than two months later, on June 16. The
termination of Quay's extended forensic effort reflected his success in securing the assurance of
higher duties, especially on iron and steel products.[38]

Yet the generally successful struggle waged by the
Republicans in behalf of protection did not include
victory in their assault against the income tax provision. Despite the existence of bipartisan opposition
against legislation regarded by creditors as prejudi-
cial to their interests,[39] the minority party proved
incapable of deleting from the bill a feature which
would later be invalidated by the Supreme Court.[40]
Without the help of Gorman, who on this phase of the
tariff measure "sacrificed his economic convictions
and his class prejudices to the need to placate other
Democrats,"[41] the Republicans failed to prevent the
passage of legislation highly objectionable to Aldrich,
Allison, Platt, Sherman, and Cullom.[42]

Nor was Republican criticism confined to the income tax provision of the Wilson-Gorman bill. Despite its drastic upward revision in the Senate, Republicans continued to make political capital of the
tariff issue by unfavorably comparing the measure of
1894 with the McKinley act of 1890. The lack of a
consistently protectionist viewpoint in the preparation
of the Democratic legislation, they argued, would result only in the perpetuation of the economic depres-

sion to a large extent ascribable to fears engendered by the free trade doctrines of the majority party.

Among the Republicans voicing dissatisfaction with the Wilson-Gorman tariff legislation was Senator Sherman, who, like Aldrich, would have preferred the continued operation of the McKinley law to the implementation of a Democratic tariff measure. This predilection Sherman made clear in a speech delivered on May 31, 1894.[43] In the act of 1890, which he regarded as a model of tariff legislation, he professed to see impartial treatment of the various sections and industries of the nation.

The Wilson-Gorman measure, on the other hand, Sherman denounced as manifesting sectional favoritism and as being so formulated as to sacrifice agricultural interests, especially those in areas outside the South. He objected to the high rates on Southern rice and peanuts, which carried duties of 84 and 73 per cent respectively, in comparison with the 20 per cent duty on grains, largely a Northern crop. The transfer of raw wool, mainly a Northern product, to the free list drew especially strong criticism from Sherman, who had many sheep-raising constituents. This provision he characterized as "the culminating atrocity" of the tariff legislation, and he declared that the action would result in an annual revenue loss of more than eight million dollars.[44] He regarded the Wilson-Gorman measure as satisfactory only in so far as its provisions coincided with those of the McKinley act. Beyond that point the Democratic tariff legislation was "decidedly sectional," incongruous, and inconsistent.[45]

So drastic was the revision of the House-approved Wilson bill that by the time the upper chamber approved the measure on July 3 raw wool and lumber were the only important products remaining on the

free list.[46] Significant among the changes effected by
the addition of 634 Senate amendments was the removal from the non-dutiable list of iron ore, coal, and
sugar. The Havemeyer interests were not to suffer
under a Democratic administration. This was made
clear by the Senate's elimination of House provisions
which had put both raw and refined sugar on the free
list, and by the imposition upon each of these products of a 40 per cent duty and an additional duty of
one-eighth cent per pound on refined sugar. These
provisions, representing the virtual dictates of the
sugar trust, served as a conspicuous example of the
manner in which protection was maintained despite
the attempts of the House to secure the enactment of
a measure even mildly in accord with professed
Democratic tariff principles.[47]

Noteworthy during the period between the Senate
passage of the Wilson-Gorman bill and its emergence
as law without the signature of the distraught Democratic President was the manner in which Reed
taunted the majority party for its abandonment of
long advocated tariff tenets. For the task of em-
phasizing the failure of the Democrats to provide the
nation with tariff legislation more in keeping with
their promises than was the Wilson-Gorman act, he
was well equipped. Reed turned to Republican advantage not only the dissension between Cleveland and
his party associates in the Senate,[48] but also the manner in which the Democratic House surrendered to
the demand of the dominant legislative branch that
the tariff measure be approved without change.

As early as July 7, when the House, in accord with
Wilson's protest over the upper chamber's disregard
for Democratic tariff principles,[49] refused to concur
in the Senate amendments, Reed had begun his attack.
The Democratic majority in the House, he cynically

predicted, would have no alternative but to accept in
entirety the Senate revisions.[50] This prophecy he reiterated on July 19, when he also sarcastically stated
that from the Republican side there would be no criticism regarding the severity with which Cleveland
castigated, in his letter to Representative Wilson, the
Democrats in the Senate.[51]

On August 13, when the House after five weeks of
delay demonstrated the accuracy of Reed's prediction
by completely capitulating to the will of the Senate,[52]
he flayed the Democratic Representatives. These
men, he asserted, were, despite their earlier declarations to the contrary, about to approve a measure
which they regarded as dishonest. Highly censurable,
in Reed's view, was the sacrifice of principle involved in the decision of the House Democrats to accept the Senate measure. Its protectionist provisions,
he pointed out, reflected such considerations as the
need for gaining votes, the prevention of interminable
filibustering, and the objective of insuring the receipt
of financial contributions from the sugar interests.
Also an object of Reed's invective was the maneuver
by which the majority leaders sought to disguise their
humiliating surrender to the upper chamber through
the useless passage of bills calling for the transfer
to the free list of iron ore, coal, barbed wire, and
sugar.[53]

Obviously the already broken Democratic party,
further weakened by its enactment of the Wilson-
Gorman bill,[54] was in no condition during the turbulent
year of 1894[55] to compete effectively with the Republicans in the biennial congressional elections. The
voters, discontented with the widespread distress and
disorder already experienced during the second
Cleveland administration, could see little point in
supporting a discordant party generally regarded as

responsible for the unsatisfactory state of affairs.
Receptive to Republican arguments "that the Democrats and hard times had come in together,"[56] the
public was willing to believe the worst concerning a
political organization whose recent tariff legislation
had been criticized by members of both parties. And
although, as Croly notes, leading Republicans, and
especially those friendly to McKinley, greatly exaggerated the Wilson-Gorman act as a factor in the
economic depression, they could "hardly be blamed"
for their attempts to take the greatest possible advantage of Democratic blundering.[57]

Aided by the recent Democratic tariff reform fias-
co, the Republicans emerged from the congressional
contests of 1894 with a sweeping majority in the House
and a plurality in the Senate.[58] Thus was the party
enabled to render increasingly vocal its contention
that in Republican protectionism lay the key to the
restoration of a prosperity conceived as the cure for
the nation's ills. In the improved position of his
party Mark Hanna detected a trend favorable to the
successful implementation of a project designed to
elevate to the presidency his protectionist minded
friend, Governor McKinley of Ohio.[59]

The jubilation of Republicans over their success
in the election of 1894 was so unrestrained as to give
rise to the boast that in the next campaign they could
elect even a rag doll to the presidency.[60] In Congress,
however, their party was disposed to inaction during
the remainder of Cleveland's second term.[61] Not until December 2, 1895 were the newly elected members admitted to that body, and despite the huge
Republican majority in the House the party was
handicapped by its possession of only a plurality in
the Senate and by the continued control of the executive department by a Democrat. Generally pleased

with the widespread criticism directed against the
Democratic administration, the majority of the Republicans were primarily concerned with achieving
success in the coming national election. In Robinson's
characterization of Reed's second term in the speakership as "merely a background for the story of the
presidential campaign of 1896"[62] is to be noted the
high degree of Republican congressional interest in
the approaching struggle.

During a period when Reed was being described as
exhibiting increased caution and amiability so as to
improve his presidential prospects,[63] the Republican
leaders were by no means averse to exploiting to the
utmost the persisting disunity within the Democratic
party. Their conduct was such as to indicate the belief that their interests could best be served by continuing to give the administration the support necessary for the maintenance of the gold standard while
indulging in the practice of criticizing the specific
methods employed.[64] The Republicans benefited from
opposition differences over the Belmont-Morgan gold
loan,[65] a transaction which aggravated the schism between the gold and silver Democrats.[66]

In late 1895 the campaign-conscious Republicans
emphasized their abiding faith in the efficacy of their
prosperity restoration argument[67] by going on record
in the Reed-managed House with the approval of a
tariff measure usually referred to as the first Dingley
bill.[68] There would appear to be little reason, however, for assuming that this action served to
strengthen protectionist Reed's position as a con-
tender for the Republican presidential nomination.
The Speaker could hardly have been expected thus to
gain sufficient publicity as an advocate of increased
tariff rates to enable him to vie successfully in the
contest for popular favor with Governor William Mc-

Kinley, whose name had long been most closely asso-
ciated with protection.

Not only did the likeable and geographically-
favored McKinley have the advantage arising from
his widespread reputation as the leading exponent of
the central feature of his party's policy. He also
stood to gain immeasurably from his good fortune in
having in charge of his presidential campaign his
mentor, Mark Hanna. As the "business man in politics," that protectionist minded Cleveland industrialist
would through his striking proficiency as an organizer
and promoter first realize in the election of 1896 his
long harbored ambition of becoming President-maker.

THE DINGLEY TARIFF

Indicative of Hanna's primary concern with promoting the interests of business was the passage during the McKinley administration of legislation increasing the tariff and giving specific legal confirmation to the gold standard. The sequence of these measures, which were intended to insure increased profits and to safeguard capital, proved disappointing to many gold men who in supporting McKinley had strongly taken to heart the emphasis given the currency question in the campaign of 1896.[1] Yet most pro-business Republicans perhaps agreed that although there was no immediate need for currency legislation,[2] there were long desired benefits to be gained from the hasty enactment of protectionist legislation regarded by Hanna and McKinley as "essential to the cure of the economic depression."[3]

The Republican leaders, in their much publicized effort to restore prosperity by replacing the allegedly faulty Democratic tariff law with one of their own making, mapped a course reflecting their decision to regard McKinley's election as a popular demand for increased protection. From their determination to give priority to protectionist legislation they had not been diverted by the stress placed during the campaign upon the monetary issue.[4] Discernible in the alacrity with which the Republican leadership displayed its protectionist preference were the pressing demands of industrialist donors eager for higher tariff duties. The manufacturers who during the campaign of 1896 h~∴ provided unprecedentedly profuse

57

pecuniary assistance to the Republican party had not, as Peck observes, been motivated by altruism. Rather, they regarded as "a strictly business investment" the money thus expended, and they viewed the launching of the new Republican administration as the occasion for receiving "full payment of their claims."[5] According to Tarbell, "Hanna knew too well what his backers in iron and steel and wool expected, and would demand for their contributions."[6]

By resorting to "a plan of action which took slight heed of precedent or of constitutional forms,"[7] the Republicans had arranged for the formulation of the new tariff bill by the expiring fifty-fourth Congress during the winter of 1896-1897. They had reached an agreement that Reed was to be re-elected to the speakership, and that the members of the Ways and Means Committee, of which Nelson Dingley of Maine was chairman, would retain their places in the new Congress.[8] Moreover, as Stanwood observes, there was undoubtedly "an understanding between the Committee and Mr. McKinley that an extraordinary session of Congress would be held almost immediately after the inauguration."[9] Thus to Dingley, the "modest man from Maine,"[10] in whom McKinley and other leading Republicans placed "implicit faith,"[11] fell the task of supervising the preparation and passage through the House of an acceptable tariff measure. The bill was expected to satisfy Hanna's protectionist desires and to represent the economic philosophy of a President-elect long regarded by the public as the foremost advocate of high tariff duties.

Nor did President McKinley choose to leave the nation in doubt concerning the administration's plan to give precedence to protectionist legislation. In his inaugural address[12] he not only expressed the view that the electorate had demanded tariff revision, but

he professed to see in the need for additional revenue
the reason for giving immediate attention to that phase
of his party's program. He expressed the view that
the contemplated tariff measure would, while protecting industry and labor, strengthen government credit,
restore confidence, and prepare the way for the future adoption of currency legislation designed to give
increased stability to the financial system. "Nothing
has ever been plainer at a general election," the
President asserted, "than that the controlling principle in the raising of revenue from duties on imports is zealous care for American interests and
American labor."

The voters, President McKinley stated, in his inaugural address, had in the election of 1896 expressed
their desire for legislation which would "give ample
protection and encouragement to the industries and
the development of our country." To that policy, he
asserted, "we are all, of whatever party, firmly
bound by the voice of the people—a power vastly more
potential than the expression of any political platform." There was immediate necessity for increased
government income, he declared. This objective
should be attained by proceeding along the line of
"settled policy" in raising the major portion of revenue through taxing imports. "The paramount duty of
Congress" was, in McKinley's judgment, "to stop de-
ficiencies by the restoration of that protective legislation which has always been the firmest prop of the
Treasury."[13]

In keeping with his desire to permit the greatest
possible dispatch in the enactment of tariff legislation,
the President in his inaugural address informed the
country of his intention to bring Congress into special
session on March 15, 1897. The friendly attitude with
which he as an exponent of legislative dominance re-

garded that body was reflected in his declaration that
he did "not sympathize with the sentiment that Congress in session is dangerous to our general business
interests." Members of that body he described as
"agents of the people," and he expressed the belief
that the presence of Congressmen at the capital should
prove beneficial to the nation.[14] The decision of the
Republican leaders to postpone the revision of the
currency system McKinley indicated by recommending the creation of a commission for the purpose of
examining that problem. Currency legislation, he declared, should not be enacted until "adequate revenue"
could be secured through the passage of a satisfactory
tariff measure.[15]

The President in thus advocating a policy embody-
ing his own protectionist predilections pointed the way
toward the development of the greatest possible degree of harmony in a party still handicapped by disunity over the silver question. For although the
House, heavily Republican,[16] was firmly opposed to
free silver, the Senate, in which the administration
held a very narrow majority, was so constituted as to
render futile any effort to secure the passage of a
gold standard measure.[17]

In accord with the purpose of promoting unity of
action,[18] McKinley charged Congress, in his extra
session message of March 15, with the single task of
enacting tariff legislation which would provide sufficient revenue.[19] He regarded as imperative expedi-
tious action in passing a measure which would raise
the funds "not only for the ordinary expenses of the
Government, but for the prompt payment of liberal
pensions and the liquidation of the principal and interest of the public debt." McKinley called for the
imposition of duties in such a manner as to assure
American producers of the greatest possible share of

"the home market," and as "to revive and increase
manufactures." He expressed the view that the proposed measure could be so applied as "to relieve and
encourage agriculture; to increase our domestic and
foreign commerce; to aid and develop mining and
building, and to render to labor in every field of useful occupation the liberal wages and adequate rewards
to which skill and industry are justly entitled."[20]

With remarkable speed did the advance preparation
of the tariff bill, the disunity among the Democrats,[21]
and the rigid Reed rules[22] permit the Republican
House to act. Introduced by Dingley on March 15,[23]
the tariff measure "was railroaded through"[24] and
passed on March 31.[25] In his sixty-minute advocacy
and explanation of the bill on March 22,[26] chairman
Dingley indicated his agreement with McKinley's
tariff views, spoke of the need for increased revenue,
and dwelled upon the alleged advantages of protection. Discernible in Dingley's discussion of the restoration of wool to the dutiable list[27] was the desire
of sound money Republican leaders to gain favor with
Western agrarians whose silverite demands had been
opposed during the electoral contest of 1896.[28]

Although in Tarbell's view "the fact seems to be
that Mr. Dingley sincerely aimed to keep duties
nearer, if possible, to the Wilson Bill than to the
McKinley Bill,"[29] the proposed measure was to a
large extent patterned after the act of 1890.[30] That
the bill as reported to the House retained practically
intact the Wilson-Gorman cotton and metal schedules
was the result, according to Dingley, of their preparation at the hands of the interested manufacturers.[31]
The action of Dingley and his associates in replacing
specific duties by ad valorem rates drew from Democrats the charge that increases on articles thus
affected had been greater than acknowledged by the

Ways and Means Committee.[32] Despite assurances by
chairman Dingley regarding the intention to avoid the
excessive rates of the McKinley law, the bill as reported included many duties equal to and some higher
than those in the legislation of 1890.[33]

So highly protectionist was the House version of
the tariff measure as to be described as "practically
the old McKinley bill" by Representative Wheeler of
Alabama, a member of the Ways and Means Committee. Congress, he complained, had been called into
session "for the purpose of enacting a tariff law, not
to increase the revenue, but for the purpose of giving
special bounties to the protected industries which
aided in the nomination and election of the present
Executive." The bill, Wheeler declared, had been
formulated by the Republicans on the committee "almost entirely from petitions" presented "by the
agents of the protected interests." He asserted that
many of the paragraphs in the measure were "almost
in the exact language of those petitions."[34]

Destined for much slower progress in the upper
than in the lower chamber, the Dingley bill was modified by the addition of 872 amendments before receiving the approval of the Senate on July 7.[35] In the
Finance Committee,[36] to which the House-approved
bill was referred on April 1, the measure underwent
revision looking toward decreased duties, and was
reported to the Senate on May 4 by Aldrich.[37]

That Senator, whose power was highly respected
by such Republican leaders as Foraker,[38] opened the
debate on the Dingley bill on May 25[39] in an address
stressing the Finance Committee's preference for a
degree of tariff reduction. Yet it was the belief of
that committee, Aldrich explained, that in no instance
had the revised rates been set under "the protective
point."[40] The committee, he declared, desired through

the practice of moderation to promote greater permanence in protectionist legislation. "Without relinquishing one particle of our devotion to the cause of protection," Aldrich stated, "we feel that we have a right to ask that the cause shall not be burdened by the imposition of duties which are unnecessary and excessive." The Finance Committee had attempted, he averred, to readjust rates in such a manner as "to make them sufficiently protective to domestic interests without being prohibitive."[41]

Aldrich's enduring solicitude for the welfare of the manufacturers was strikingly revealed in his upward revision of the sugar duties.[42] That schedule embodied an increase in rates effected by a combination of specifics and ad valorems so complicated that at the conclusion of his lengthy explanation of the proposed scheme "everybody knew less than before."[43] The plan, regarded by Taussig as "difficult to explain except as a means of making concessions under disguise to the refiners,"[44] raised "an immediate cry that Mr. Aldrich was trying to play into the hands of the sugar trust."[45] This feature of the legislation appears to have played a part in the return of the bill to the Finance Committee and in the replacement of Aldrich by Allison in the task of managing the tariff measure in the Senate.[46]

Reflected in the generally increased rates written into the Dingley bill following Allison's succession to Aldrich as the manager of the measure was the effective pressure exerted by the silver Republican Senators for higher duties on wool, hides, and lead.[47] For this segment of the narrowly Republican Senate was in a strategic position both in the Finance Committee, in which Jones of Nevada wielded great influence,[48] and on the floor. In the belief that the measure could be saved only through granting the concessions de-

manded by the silverites, the Republican leaders
sanctioned amendments resulting in the establishment
of duties generally above those approved by the
House.[49]   Although much responsibility for increased
rates has been placed upon the silver Republicans,
Peck points out that "a number of Senators, who
represented the great corporations and the manufacturers, interposed on behalf of their friends and
benefactors."[50]

Nor did the upward modification to which the Dingley bill was subjected in the Senate cease with the
passage of the measure by that body on July 7. In the
conference committee[51] to which the legislation was
referred following the refusal of the House to concur
in the upper chamber's amendments to the bill, the
duties were raised to a level generally above that
approved by either branch.[52] Presented by Dingley
to the House on July 19,[53] the conference report gained
the approval of that body by a vote of 187 to 116 and
on July 24 was ratified by the Senate with 40 affirma-
tive as against 30 negative votes.[54] And such was the
celerity with which the protectionist President per-
formed his part in putting into effect the tariff legislation whose average rate reached the highest level
yet attained[55] that not a day elapsed before his signature was on the measure.[56]

Yet despite his apparent eagerness for increased
rates, McKinley had in the period following the election of 1896 indicated a reconsideration of his longtime advocacy of ever higher duties. His elevation
to the presidency had been, with justification, regarded as constituting an assurance that the nation's
business men would be greatly favored in the White
House. He had revealed, however, at the time of his
appointment of Lyman Gage as Secretary of the
Treasury, a belief in the advisability of a gradual re-

duction in tariff rates to a level lower than that established by the act of 1890.[57] Moreover, McKinley's sincere though largely futile effort to promote reciprocity in accord with the platform pledge of 1896,[58] and as provided for in the tariff act of 1897, reflected his maturing judgment that industry no longer required the extreme protection for which he had so zealously pleaded.[59]

Yet so highly restrictive were the reciprocity provisions included in an act formulated primarily for the benefit of industry that their effective implementation was prevented.[60] From the power granted the President, in the third section of the law, to proclaim a reduction of duties on specified articles[61] only insignificant concessions were obtained.[62] Nor was any appreciable degree of success achieved through the provision in the fourth section of the measure authorizing the President to negotiate treaties calling for duty reductions of as much as 20 per cent. As a consequence of the provision limiting to two years the time allowed for the conclusion of such treaties, and of the requirement that they must be "ratified by the Senate and approved by Congress,"[63] protectionists were enabled to render nugatory the reciprocity sections of the act.

Although President McKinley energetically promoted the negotiation of a number of such agreements,[64] they failed to gain the approval of the Senate. These treaties, as Cullom, a member of the upper chamber favoring them observes, were destined to failure because of the bitter opposition on the part of such unsympathetic solons as Aldrich and Hanna.[65] Cullom condemns as "a very short-sighted policy" the insistence of these leaders that the treaties in question "should be killed."[66] As much of the support accorded the Dingley tariff bill reflected the belief of many Congressmen that decreased duties would be effected through the conclusion of reciprocity agreements, their obstruction by the Senate could, in Muzzey's view, "hardly be characterized as other than a breach of faith."[67]

As a result of the highly protectionist nature of the Dingley act, according to Taussig, "even good party members, loyal to the general policy of protection, doubted whether that policy had not now been carried too far."[68] Considerations of this type, however, served neither to prevent such Senators as Hanna and Aldrich from resisting tariff reduction, nor to restrain President McKinley from hastily signing the measure. This legislation, heartily approved by Hanna,[69] represented "the outcome of an aggressive spirit of protection"[70] and constituted the greatest tariff triumph yet achieved by the forces of business.[71]

Through a combination of factors including the long tenure of power by the Republicans and the direction of public attention to such developments as the Spanish-American War and imperialism, the Dingley act was assured of a long life. This legislation, whose adoption was accompanied by the beginning of prosperity, provoked no public reaction similar to that earlier occasioned by the McKinley law.[72] And although this prosperity was effected despite, rather than as a result of, the Dingley act,[73] so well contented were Americans with it that in the presidential contest of 1900 the tariff was not regarded as an issue of even secondary importance.[74]

NOTES - PROTECTION FOR INDUSTRIALISTS:
THE POST-CIVIL WAR YEARS

1. See Herbert Croly, Marcus Alonzo Hanna: His Life and Work (New York, 1912), 418.

2. Faulkner notes that "The Act of 1857 reduced the maximum protection to 24 per cent and the general level of duties was reduced to the lowest point since 1815." Harold Underwood Faulkner, American Economic History (5th ed., New York, 1943), 536. See also William J. Shultz and C. Lowell Harriss, American Public Finance (5th ed., New York, 1949), 514-15.

3. See F. W. Taussig, The Tariff History of the United States (5th ed., New York, 1901), 158-60; Faulkner, Economic History, 536.

4. Stephen Enke and Virgil Salera, International Economics (New York, 1947), 506. Taussig notes that the war tariff of 1864, the important features of which remained in effect for almost two decades and provided the basis for even higher protection, "raised duties greatly and indiscriminately," increasing the average level from 37.2 per cent as provided by the measure of 1862 to 47.06 per cent. "In many ways crude and ill-considered," he adds, the act of 1864 "established protective duties more extreme than had been ventured on in any previous tariff act in our country's history; it contained flagrant abuses, in the shape of duties whose chief effect was to bring money into the pockets of private individuals." Taussig, Tariff History, 167, 170.

5. See Broadus Mitchell and Louise Pearson Mitchell, American Economic History (Chicago, 1947), 744.

6. See ibid., 742.

7. See Shultz and Harriss, Public Finance, 515.

8. Mitchell and Mitchell, Economic History, 742. Kirkland states that "the interests that were benefited or thought they were benefited from the continuance of high rates were successful in preventing any sweeping general reduction." Edward C. Kirkland, A History of American Economic Life (rev. ed., New York, 1939), 409. Poole points out that in the period following the Civil War "the tariff remained the major revenue source, customs accounting for 55-60 per cent of total Federal revenues in the decade 1880-1890." Kenyon Edwards Poole (ed.), Fiscal Policies and the American Economy (New York, 1951), 18.

9. Tarbell states that "There was something devout, as well as childlike, in McKinley's devotion to the dogma." Ida M. Tarbell, The Nationalizing of Business, 1878-1898, Vol. IX of A History of American Life (New York, 1936), 195. See also Ida M. Tarbell, The Tariff in Our Times (New York, 1911), 186; David Saville Muzzey, The United States of America (2 vols., Boston, 1924), II, 200.

10. Charles S. Olcott, The Life of William McKinley (2 vols., Boston, 1916), I, 130. Frederic Logan Paxson, "William McKinley," Dictionary of American Biography, ed. by Allen Johnson, Dumas Malone, and Harris E. Starr (21 vols., New York, 1928-1944), XII, 105.

11. Tarbell notes in connection with McKinley's congressional service that "his chief interest had always been the tariff." Tarbell, Nationalizing of Business, 195.

12. Tarbell, Tariff, 186.

13. Representative William D. Kelley's tireless efforts in the House since 1861 in seeking high duties for iron and steel had gained him the appellation, "Pig

Iron." Olcott, McKinley, I, 137; Murat Halstead, Life and Distinguished Services of William McKinley, Our Martyr President (Memorial Association Publishers, 1901), 69.

14. Olcott, McKinley, I, 138.

15. Muzzey, United States, II, 200. In 1880 McKinley replaced Garfield on the Ways and Means Committee. Cong. Record, 46 Cong., 3 Sess., 281 (December 20, 1880); Paxson, op. cit., XII, 105.

16. For McKinley's address see Cong. Record, 45 Cong., 2 Sess., 2541-46 (April 15, 1878). See also Joseph P. Smith (comp.), Speeches and Addresses of William McKinley from His Election to Congress to the Present Time (New York, 1893), 1-22. "It was really a wonderful speech," declares Halstead, "and it made the young Congressman . . . a figure in the House." This speech, Halstead states, indicated the presence of "a new force" in Congress. Halstead, McKinley, 66-67.

17. Tarbell, Tariff, 88.

18. In 1881 and 1882 the surplus rose to a hundred million dollars. See Faulkner, Economic History, 538; Ernest L. Bogart and Donald L. Kemmerer, Economic History of the American People (New York, 1947), 446.

19. Cong. Record, 47 Cong., 1 Sess., 2659-69 (April 6, 1882); Smith (comp.), Speeches of McKinley, 70-105.

20. The president of the commission was John L. Hayes, secretary of the Wool Manufacturers' Association. See Taussig, Tariff History, 231; Davis Rich Dewey, Financial History of the United States (8th ed., London, 1922), 420-21; Mitchell and Mitchell, Economic History, 745.

21. "Our laborers," McKinley declared, "are not only the best paid, clothed, and educated in the world, but

they have more comforts, more independence, more of them live in the houses they own, more of them have money in savings institutions, and are better contented than their rivals anywhere else." Cong. Record, 47 Cong., 1 Sess., 2660; Smith (comp.), Speeches of McKinley, 74.

22. See Arthur Cecil Bining, The Rise of American Economic Life (New York, 1943), 364. The commission's recommendations "applied to commodities of necessary general consumption, to sugar and molasses, rather than to luxuries, and to raw rather than to manufactured materials." Dewey, Financial History, 420-21.

23. The legislation was passed by the Republican lame duck House just prior to the relinquishment of its control to the Democrats. Matthew Josephson, The Politicos, 1865-1896 (New York, 1938), 333. See also Faulkner, Economic History, 538; Bogart and Kemmerer, Economic History, 446.

24. See Mitchell and Mitchell, Economic History, 745-46; Taussig, Tariff History, 231-33.

25. Dewey, Financial History, 424.

26. In this connection see Halstead, McKinley, 70.

27. Aldrich had previously been elected to Congress in 1878 and 1880. In the Senate he replaced the deceased General Burnside. See Nathaniel Wright Stephenson, Nelson W. Aldrich: A Leader in American Politics (New York, 1930), 35-40.

28. The chief strength of Aldrich, whose business activities included a partnership in a wholesale grocery firm and the presidency of a bank and of a street railway company, emanated from "his appeal to the business classes," and as Senator he chose to regard himself as representing "an economic constituency." Stephenson, Aldrich, 8, 35, 59-61. See also Henry Beech Needham, "The Senate—of 'Special Interests,'"

World's Work (New York) XI (January, 1906), 7064-
65, (February, 1906), 7208; Lincoln Steffens, "Rhode
Island: A State for Sale, What Senator Aldrich Represents—A Business Man's Government Founded
upon the Corruption of the People Themselves," Mc-
Clure's Magazine (New York), XXIV (February,
1905), 337, 347-50; David Graham Phillips, "The
Treason of the Senate," Cosmopolitan Magazine (New
York), XL (April, 1906), 630.

29. Nathaniel Wright Stephenson, "Nelson Wilmarth
Aldrich," Dictionary of American Biography, I, 152,
153. See also Shelby M. Cullom, Fifty Years of
Public Service (2d ed., Chicago, 1911), 209.

30. "It was not only the people below the average, it was
the whole vast congregation of the easily led, the
easily deceived, the easily betrayed people, that
roused his scorn. But it was not his way ever to have
direct dealings with them. He would not even dis-
abuse them when they misunderstood him." Stephenson, Aldrich, 61. According to Barry, Aldrich
firmly believed that the people neither knew "what
they wanted in a legislative way" nor "what was good
for them." It was as "so much trash" that he regarded the portion of his mail consisting of unsolicited suggestions. David S. Barry, Forty Years in
Washington (Boston, 1924), 160.

31. Stephenson, Aldrich, 94.

32. Ibid., 50; Josephson, Politicos, 329. See also Phillips, op. cit., XL, 632, 636.

33. Steffens, op. cit., XXIV, 347.

34. On February 6, 1883 Aldrich noted that the membership of the tariff commission included representatives of the iron and sugar interests and that "those
interests were very carefully looked out for and pre-
served." Cong. Record, 47 Cong., 2 Sess., 2149
(February 6, 1883). "It was said on the inside," ac-

cording to Tarbell, that Aldrich "was the man who had written the cotton schedule for the report of the Tariff Commission." Tarbell, Tariff, 111.

35. Ibid., 169. Stanwood states that Aldrich probably possessed "a wider and deeper knowledge of the tariff in all its details, and in its relations to business, commerce, and manufactures, than any other man who ever served in Congress." Edward Stanwood, American Tariff Controversies in the Nineteenth Century (2 vols., Boston, 1903), II, 263.

36. Stephenson, Aldrich, 50-51.

37. Ibid., 49.

38. Taussig, Tariff History, 232.

39. Stephenson, Aldrich, 49.

40. Ibid., 50; Cong. Record, 50 Cong., 1 Sess., 9549-50 (October 18, 1888); 2 Sess., 452, 455 (January 2, 1889), 625 (January 9, 1889).

41. Tarbell, Tariff, 169. In regard to the increased recognition being accorded by legislators to business men in the devising of duties, Tarbell notes that although the latter "had been more or less active in every bill since the war . . . never before had their right to stand day and night at the doors of Senate and House, to sit in committee, to be closeted in every leisure hour with their representatives in Congress, been conceded. It was recognition they were not likely to forget." Ibid., 131-32.

42. See ibid., 169; Dewey, Financial History, 396.

43. Sherman was born in 1823, Allison in 1829, Aldrich in 1841, and McKinley in 1843. Sherman was first elected to the House in 1854, eight years prior to Allison's election to that chamber. See John Sherman, Recollections of Forty Years in the House, Senate and Cabinet: An Autobiography (2 vols., Chicago, 1895), I, 105; Arthur Wallace Dunn, "Senator

Allison's Recollections of Public Men," Review of Reviews (New York) XXXIX (May, 1909), 555; Leland L. Sage, William Boyd Allison: A Study in Practical Politics (Iowa City, 1956), 2-58.

44. See Dewey, Financial History, 396.

45. Cong. Globe, 41 Cong., 2 Sess., Appendix, 193, 198 (March 25, 1870). See also Tarbell, Tariff, 67, 165-66; "The Presidency and Senator Allison," Atlantic Monthly (Boston) LXXVII (April, 1896), 547; Sage, Allison, 103.

46. Tarbell, Tariff, 75-76.

47. See ibid., 51.

48. Ibid., 165-66; Jeanette P. Nichols, "William Boyd Allison," Dictionary of American Biography, I, 220, 221; Jeanette P. Nichols, "John Sherman," ibid., XVII, 85, 87. See also Sherman, Recollections, II, 1088-89, 1127-29, 1165; Winfield S. Kerr, John Sherman: His Life and Public Service (2 vols., Boston, 1908), II, 275; "Senator Allison," Nation, LXXXVII (August 13, 1908), 133.

49. In regard to Sherman's support of the legislation creating the Tariff Commission, see Sherman, Recollections, II, 841-43.

50. Ibid., 851-55.

51. Ibid., 852.

52. Stephenson states that Sherman "cleared his skirts by loading upon Aldrich the whole responsibility for the wool tariff." Stephenson, Aldrich, 61. See also ibid., note 21, 432; Sherman, Recollections, II, 851, 853-54.

53. Ibid., 843.

54. Dewey, Financial History, 424; Katherine Coman, The Industrial History of the United States (New York, 1930), 315.

55. This bill, which called for reductions averaging 20 per cent and provided for enlarging the free list, was defeated in the House on May 6 by a vote of 156 to 151. Morrison's somewhat different proposal of 1886, which provided for the inclusion in the free list of wool, lumber, flax, and hemp, failed to gain House consideration. See Dewey, Financial History, 423; Davis Rich Dewey, National Problems, 1885-1897, Vol. XXIV of The American Nation: A History (New York, 1907), 61-62; Taussig, Tariff History, 251-52.

56. Halstead, McKinley, 71; Cong. Record, 48 Cong., 1 Sess., Appendix, 134-41 (April 30, 1884). True Americans, McKinley asserted, did not favor this tariff bill. Producers of iron, steel, glass, woolens, and cottons he described as benefactors who in general did not represent the wealthy classes. The continuation of prosperity required the maintenance of the protective system, and enactment of the proposed measure would be a step in the destruction of the national economic structure.

57. James D. Richardson (ed), A Compilation of the Messages and Papers of the Presidents, 1789-1897 (10 vols., Washington, 1896-99), VIII, 580-91.

58. See Dewey, Financial History, 423-24; Dewey, National Problems, 64; Sherman, Recollections, II, 1004-1005.

59. See Faulkner, Economic History, 538.

60. Tarbell, Tariff, 152.

61. See David Saville Muzzey, James G. Blaine: A Political Idol of Other Days (New York, 1934), 366-67; Public Opinion (Washington), IV (December 17, 1887), 217-21.

62. See Smith (comp.), Speeches of McKinley, 250-62, "Address before the Home Market Club, at Banquet in Hotel Vendome, Boston, Mass., February 9, 1888."

63. House Report No. 1496 (Serial 2602) 50 Cong., 1
Sess., 17-18 (April 2, 1888); William McKinley, A
History of Tariff Legislation from 1812 to 1896, Vol.
VII of Works of Henry Clay, Comprising His Life,
Correspondence and Speeches, ed. by Calvin Colton
(New York, 1897), 184.

64. The proposed average reduction of only about 7 per
cent, intended to reduce the average level from 47 to
40 per cent represented, according to Dewey, "a
paltry difference when measured by the tests of the
president's message." In defending the measure,
Dewey notes, the Democrats "harped upon the fact
that the Mills bill decreased tariff duties by an average of only 7 per cent, and that their recommendations were in harmony with those made earlier by
Republicans." Dewey, National Problems, 67, 69.
The bill, named after chairman Roger Q. Mills of the
Ways and Means Committee, called for slight reductions on finished goods, and provided for cheap
or free raw materials such as hemp, lumber, flax,
and wool. See Taussig, Tariff History, 254-55; Ellis
Paxson Oberholtzer, A History of the United States
Since the Civil War (5 vols., New York, 1917-1937),
IV, 488; Tarbell, Tariff, 159; Josephson, Politicos,
402-403.

65. Republican criticisms included the charges that the
measure had been prepared without permitting hearings to interested industrialists, without allowing
participation by the minority party members, and
without granting adequate public hearings. The measure was also attacked as revealing sectional favoritism. See Smith (comp.), Speeches of McKinley,
277-89; Stanwood, Tariff Controversies, II, 231-32;
Tarbell, Tariff, 179.

66. See Taussig, Tariff History, 254. Cullom states,
"We all thought it incumbent upon us to make
speeches for home consumption for campaign use,
showing the iniquities of the Mills bill and of the

Democratic tariff generally, although we knew it was impossible for either bill to become law." Cullom, Fifty Years, 244. See also Tarbell, Tariff, 178.

67. In addition to denouncing the Mills bill in their platform of 1888, the Republicans described themselves as being "uncompromisingly in favor of the American system of protection," and they "heartily" endorsed "the consistent and patriotic action of the Republican Representatives in Congress in opposing" the passage of the measure. In their support of the protectionist system the Republicans protested "against its destruction as proposed by the President and his party." "The Republican party," the platform asserted, "would effect all needed reduction of the National revenue by repealing the taxes upon tobacco . . . and the tax upon spirits used in the arts, and for mechanical purposes, and by such revision of the tariff laws as will tend to check the imports of such articles as are produced by our people, the production of which gives employment to our labor, and releases from import duties those articles of foreign production (except luxuries), the like of which cannot be produced at home." Kirk H. Porter (comp.), National Party Platforms (New York, 1924), 147, 148; Thomas Hudson McKee (ed.), The National Conventions and Platforms of all Political Parties, 1789 to 1901 (4th ed., Baltimore, 1901), 240. See also Dewey, Financial History, 425.

68. In regard to the so-called "Great Debate," which included 151 speeches, see Stanwood, Tariff Controversies, II, 234.

69. See Cullom, Fifty Years, 243.

70. Cong. Record, 50 Cong., 1 Sess., 4400-4411 (May 18, 1888); Smith (comp.), Speeches of McKinley, 290-335.

71. Olcott, McKinley, I, 149-50.

72. "The honors," Robinson states, "were generally

accorded to Reed." William A. Robinson, Thomas B. Reed: Parliamentarian (New York, 1930), 180.

73. Reed, whose speeches seldom lasted longer than a quarter of an hour, made the first important protectionist speech of his congressional career on February 3, 1883. Ibid., 94, 178; Cong. Record, 47 Cong., 2 Sess., 2055 (February 3, 1883).

74. Robinson, Reed, 35-36, 94.

75. Josephson, Politicos, 328-29.

76. Robinson, Reed, 94-95; Taussig, Tariff History, note 1, 232. See also George B. Galloway, Congress at the Crossroads (New York, 1946), 131.

77. Cong. Record, 50 Cong., 1 Sess., 4440-46 (May 19, 1888); Robinson, Reed, 172, 178-81.

78. Reed was 6 feet, 3 inches tall. Ernest Sutherland Bates, The Story of Congress, 1789-1935 (New York, 1936), 301. According to Lodge, Reed was a "most effective debater" with great ability for briefly "stating a case unanswerably," a master of ridicule able to employ "wit and sarcasm which cut and scarred when it fell like the lash of a whip." Henry Cabot Lodge, The Democracy of the Constitution, and Other Addresses and Essays (New York, 1915), 197-99.

79. Stephenson, Aldrich, 70.

80. Tarbell, Tariff, 170.

81. See Taussig, Tariff History, 255; Tarbell, Tariff, 169.

82. See Josephson, Politicos, 404; Tarbell, Tariff, 173-74.

83. Ibid., 172-73; Tarbell, Nationalizing of Business, 194. There were charges that the Senate substitute was utilized in that body throughout the campaign "in order to make deals with manufacturers who

might be induced to contribute to campaign funds."
Stephenson, <u>Aldrich</u>, note 11, 435.

84. Morrill to Aldrich, October 6, 1888, quoted in Stephenson, <u>Aldrich</u>, 73.

85. "By 1888," Tarbell states, Aldrich "had indeed become more influential than either Sherman or Allison." Tarbell, <u>Tariff</u>, 169. See also Stephenson, <u>Aldrich</u>, 70; Cullom, <u>Fifty Years</u>, 209.

86. The majority report of the Finance Committee was published for use in the campaign. Stephenson, <u>Aldrich</u>, 73.

87. <u>Cong. Record</u>, 50 Cong., 1 Sess., 9109 (October 3, 1888). See also Tarbell, <u>Tariff</u>, 165, 168; Sage, <u>Allison</u>, 232.

88. See Stephenson, <u>Aldrich</u>, 70, 73.

89. The Senate substitute, not yet passed by that body when Congress adjourned on October 20, failed to gain Senate approval until the following January 22. The measure died in the House following a report by the Ways and Means Committee branding the substitute as unconstitutional because it was not an amendment to the Mills bill, as pretended by the Senate, but rather a new revenue measure, which the upper chamber was not authorized to originate. Oberholtzer, <u>History</u>, IV, 491; Tarbell, <u>Tariff</u>, 181-84; Stanwood, <u>Tariff Controversies</u>, II, 241-42; Sherman, <u>Recollections</u>, II, 1009-10.

90. See <u>Public Opinion</u>, V (September 15, 1888), 490-92.

91. Charles Hedges (comp.), <u>Speeches of Benjamin Harrison</u> (New York, 1892), 179.

92. <u>Ibid.</u>, 157-58.

93. <u>Ibid.</u>, 66, 68.

94. <u>Ibid.</u>, 110.

95. Ibid., 178.

96. Ibid., 88-89, 168.

97. Ibid., 60, 96, 99.

98. Ibid., 85, 100, 133.

99. Ibid., 133. Harrison referred to himself as "one of those uninstructed political economists" who believed "that some things may be too cheap," and he declared that to him the "demand for cheaper coats" seemed "necessarily to involve a cheaper man and woman under the coat." Quoted in "The Mugwump Justification," Nation (New York), XLVII (July 5, 1888), 4.

100. Hedges (comp.), Speeches of Harrison, 85.

101. Ibid., 179.

102. Stanwood, Tariff Controversies, II, 240-41. For similar opinions see Muzzey, Blaine, 440; Percy Ashley, Modern Tariff History, Germany--United States--France (3d ed., New York, 1926), 198; Taussig, Tariff History, 255.

103. Samuel Eliot Morison and Henry Steele Commager, The Growth of the American Republic (2 vols., 4th ed., New York, 1951), II, 234; Fred Albert Shannon, Economic History of the People of the United States (New York, 1934), 578-79; Arthur N. Holcombe, The Political Parties of Today: A Study in Republican and Democratic Politics (New York, 1924), 207-208.

104. Arthur Wallace Dunn, From Harrison to Harding: A Personal Narrative, Covering a Third of a Century, 1888-1921 (2 vols., New York, 1922), I, 46.

105. Alexander Dana Noyes, Thirty Years of American Finance: A Short Financial History of the Government and People of the United States Since the Civil War, 1865-1896 (New York, 1901), 131; Alexander Dana Noyes, Forty Years of American Finance: A Short Financial History of the Government and People

of the United States Since the Civil War, 1865-1907
(New York, 1909), 131. Taussig calls attention to the
Senate substitute of 1888 as an indication of the Republican intention to increase the tariff rates. Taussig, Tariff History, 256.

106. In the Senate the Republicans outnumbered the Democrats by a membership of 47 to 37. In the House the
count was 166 to 159. Muzzey, United States, II, 196.
See also Oberholtzer, History, V, 104; Stanwood,
Tariff Controversies, II, 257-58.

107. Harrison to Blaine, February 11, 1889, quoted in
Stephenson, Aldrich, 77. Stephenson views as a
major mistake Harrison's refusal to follow Blaine's
advice in this connection. See also ibid., notes 3 and
4, 435-36.

108. See Muzzey, United States, II, 197.

109. Harrison represented Indiana in the United States
Senate from 1881 to 1887. He was defeated in his
attempt to secure re-election.

110. Dunn, Harrison to Harding, I, 41.

111. In a campaign speech at Indianapolis on June 26,
1888 Harrison referred to Sherman as one of the
"old-time leaders of the Republican party" whose
qualifications for the presidency surpassed those of
the man selected by the convention. Hedges (comp.),
Speeches of Harrison, 30. In a letter to Sherman,
Harrison referred to himself as "an inexperienced
politician as well as statesman" and in seeking
Sherman's assistance declared, "I have always said
to all friends that your equipment for the presidency
was so ample and your services to the party so great
that I felt there was a sort of inappropriateness in
passing you by for any of us." Harrison to Sherman,
July 9, 1888, Sherman, Recollections, II, 1030.

112. Sherman to Harrison, November 26, 1888, ibid., 1032.

113. See Muzzey, United States, II, 197.

NOTES - THE MCKINLEY TARIFF

1. Richardson (ed.), Messages, IX, 5-14; Renzo D. Bowers (ed.), The Inaugural Addresses of the Presidents (St. Louis, 1929), 308-23.

2. Richardson (ed.), Messages, IX, 32-58.

3. Ibid., 12.

4. Ibid., 39.

5. Ibid., 39.

6. Noyes, American Finance, 132-33.

7. Brown notes that "With the exception of the Forty-Seventh Congress [1881-1883], Democratic speakers had presided over the House since 1875." George Rothwell Brown, The Leadership of Congress (Indianapolis, 1922), 84.

8. M. P. Follett, The Speaker of the House of Representatives (New York, 1896), 187. See also W. F. Willoughby, Principles of Legislative Organization and Administration (Washington, 1934), 482.

9. Ibid., 481. See also Galloway, Congress at Crossroads, 131; James Ford Rhodes, History of the United States from the Compromise of 1850 (9 vols., New York, 1893-1919), VII, 342; Stanwood, Tariff Controversies, II, 258; Robinson, Reed, 175-86.

10. Samuel W. McCall, The Life of Thomas Brackett Reed (Boston, 1914), 165-66. See also Robinson, Reed, 204, 207.

11. Brown, Leadership of Congress, 97-98.

12. Robinson, Reed, 78.

13. In a House speech on January 28, 1880 Reed had defended the traditionally accepted view that the determination of a quorum was to be based not upon the actual presence of Representatives but rather upon their willingness formally to acknowledge their presence. In 1882 he again took this stand. See Robinson, Reed, 68-69, 205; McCall, Reed, 81-82; Cong. Record, 46 Cong., 2 Sess., 578-79 (January 28, 1880).

14. See Robinson, Reed, 186-92.

15. Lodge, Democracy, 197. McCall states that Reed "soon became unequaled as a parliamentarian, not perhaps in his definite knowledge of the numerous precedents in the history of the House, but in his broad comprehension of its workings and of the anatomy of its structure." McCall, Reed, 80. See also Robinson, Reed, 64.

16. Supra, 14.

17. Reed acted in this capacity from 1885 to 1889 and from 1891 to 1895, years during which the Democrats controlled the lower chamber.

18. Reed, solidly supported at the outset of the contest by the New England Representatives, was elevated to the position when on December 2, 1889 the House Republicans ratified the narrow victory accorded him by the caucus on November 30, when he had received 85 of the 166 votes as against 38 for McKinley, 19 for Cannon, 14 for Henderson, and 10 for Burrows. Reed's success was achieved despite the efforts of Hanna in behalf of McKinley. Robinson, Reed, 197-98; McCall, Reed, 162-63; Croly, Hanna, 150; Olcott, McKinley, I, 152-53.

19. See Robinson, Reed, 235; Olcott, McKinley, I, 153.

20. Robinson, Reed, 229.

21. See McCall, Reed, 166; Robinson, Reed, 220; Paul

De Witt Hasbrouck, Party Government in the House of Representatives (New York, 1927), 1.

22. Robinson, Reed, 219-20.

23. In response to Crisp's declaration of "No Quorum," following the completion of a roll call taken during the consideration of a contested election and answered by only 163 of the assembled Representatives, the Speaker asserted that "The Chair directs the Clerk to record the following names of members present and refusing to vote." Reed replied to a denial, by McCreary, of the Speaker's right to count as present a silent member with the declaration that "The Chair is making a statement of the fact that the gentleman from Kentucky is present. Does he deny it?" Cong. Record, 51 Cong., 1 Sess., 949 (January 29, 1890). See also Robinson, Reed, 208-209; McCall, Reed, 167-68; Public Opinion, VII (May 4, 1889), 74; VIII (February 8, 1890), 420, (February 22, 1890), 467. In the contested West Virginia election case of Smith v. Jackson, the Republican, Smith, was seated. See Robinson, Reed, 207, 217-18, 220.

24. A. Maurice Low, "The Oligarchy of the Senate," North American Review (New York) CLXXIV (February, 1902), 234. See also Paul S. Reinsch (ed.), Readings on American Federal Government (Boston, 1909), 148. In regard to the admittedly unprecedented nature of Reed's ruling, see McCall, Reed, 169; Robinson, Reed, 210; Willoughby, Legislative Organization, 483.

25. In explaining his ruling Reed called attention to the constitutional provision empowering the House to devise rules to compel attendance, maintaining that this section would be worthless if Representatives attending could avoid being counted for quorums by failure to participate in the proceedings. The constitutional provision, he had come to believe, provided not for a voting but for a present quorum.

Cong. Record, 51 Cong., 1 Sess., 950-51 (January 29, 1890); Robinson, Reed, 210; McCall, Reed, 169.

26. Robinson, Reed, 208-17; McCall, Reed, 167-69.

27. Willoughby, Legislative Organization, 483.

28. McCall, Reed, 170-71.

29. Robinson, Reed, 217-18.

30. Ibid., 219, 223-31. See also McCall, Reed, 170-71; Willoughby, Legislative Organization, 484; William A. Robinson, "Thomas Brackett Reed," Dictionary of American Biography, XV, 458.

31. Robinson, Reed, 227.

32. See Brown, Leadership of Congress, 97. Recognition of this aspect of Reed's services need not obscure the value of his contribution in establishing a system permitting the House to function as a legislative body. Galloway states that "Reed's rulings were eminently designed to prevent anarchistic filibustering," and Low chooses to describe them as "absolutely necessary." Robinson and McCall stress the importance of Reed's contribution by calling attention to the subsequent Democratic adoption of his quorum rule under pressure of his dilatory demonstrations during the fifty-third Congress. Galloway, Congress at Crossroads, 132; Low, op. cit., CLXXIV, 234; Robinson, Reed, 296-304; McCall, Reed, 80, 171-72.

33. Brown, Leadership of Congress, 84-85. The assignment of McKinley to this committee is described by Olcott as "an appointment of epoch-making moment." Cannon, who was placed on the Appropriations Committee, also served along with McKinley on the Rules Committee, which was headed by Reed. Olcott, McKinley, I, 154; Robinson, Reed, 199; Brown, Leadership of Congress, 85.

34. Robinson, who states that Reed held McKinley "in no exalted estimation," declares that from an intellectual standpoint McKinley was "far inferior to Reed." Robinson, Reed, 200.

35. Ibid., 237-38.

36. Ibid., 200; Brown, Leadership of Congress, 84; Croly, Hanna, 150; Clarence A. Stern, Resurgent Republicanism: The Handiwork of Hanna (Ann Arbor, 1968), 1-19.

37. Robinson, Reed, 326.

38. Ibid., 200.

39. Bates notes that Reed "was accused of counting even those in the halls and washrooms when necessary," and Muzzey states that the Speaker's arbitrary conduct was regarded as dangerous to constitutional rights. Bates, Congress, 301; Muzzey, United States, II, 213. Peck states that under Reed's management of the House, appeals from rulings by the chair were not recognized, nor were minority members allowed to question the count made by the Speaker who recorded as being in attendance Representatives who were really many miles distant from Washington. To such lengths did Reed's tyranny proceed that on June 19, 1890 a number of Republicans joined the Democrats in overriding his refusal to permit the correction of portions of the House journal containing "a record of proceedings which had never taken place." Harry Thurston Peck, Twenty Years of the Republic, 1885-1905 (New York, 1907), 213-14; Cong. Record, 51 Cong., 1 Sess., 6261-62 (June 19, 1890).

40. Robinson, Reed, 324-25.

41. Ibid., 200.

42. Croly, Hanna, 150.

43. Peck, Twenty Years, 208-209.

44. Olcott, McKinley, I, 156-57. Olcott states that Mc-
    Kinley "knew what he wanted in every particular and
    usually secured it," and that in the process he uti-
    lized "the knowledge of many minds, not only in the
    committee but outside of Congress." Ibid., 156-57.
    Stanwood describes the Ways and Means Committee
    as "one of the strongest committees ever consti-
    tuted." In addition to McKinley the Republican mem-
    bers included Representatives Nelson Dingley, Jr.
    (Maine), Thomas M. Bayne (Pennsylvania), Sereno E.
    Payne (New York), Julius C. Burrows (Michigan),
    John H. Gear (Iowa), Robert M. LaFollette (Wiscon-
    sin), and Joseph E. McKenna (California). Stanwood,
    Tariff Controversies, II, 259-60. See also McKinley,
    Tariff Legislation, 101; Cong. Directory, 51 Cong.,
    1 Sess., 137. In regard to McKinley's recognition of
    the able assistance of Dingley in the formulation of
    the tariff legislation of 1890, see Edward Nelson
    Dingley, The Life and Times of Nelson Dingley, Jr.
    (Kalamazoo, 1902), 325. See also Robinson, Reed,
    200.

45. Dewey, Financial History, 438; Tarbell, Tariff, 188;
    Sherman, Recollections, II, 1086.

46. Stephenson, Aldrich, 82-83.

47. See Tarbell, Tariff, 188; Stanwood, Tariff Contro-
    versies, II, 261.

48. Oberholtzer, History, V, 107. See also "Hearings on
    the Tariff," Nation, L (January 2, 1890), 4.

49. Although April 16 was the date that McKinley re-
    ported the bill, it was not subjected to discussion
    until May 7, when, according to him, "it was deter-
    mined to limit general debate to four days, in the
    Committee of the Whole, and then allow eight days
    for consideration, section by section, under the five-
    minute rule." McKinley, Tariff Legislation, 106.
    See also Oberholtzer, History, V, 108.

50. Tarbell, Tariff, 187-88.

51. Stanwood, Tariff Controversies, II, 261.

52. McKinley, Tariff Legislation, 106. See also Stanwood, Tariff Controversies, II, 261.

53. Rhodes, History, VIII, 347-48. See also Peck, Twenty Years, 210; Oberholtzer, History, V, 107.

54. McKinley, Tariff Legislation, 106-27. Earlier, on December 17, McKinley had introduced a Customs Administration bill designed to prevent evasion of the payment of duties and providing for a board of appraisers to determine questions of valuation and classification. In the face of considerable Democratic opposition this measure was enacted by a strict Republican vote and was approved by President Harrison on June 10, 1890. See ibid., 103-104; Olcott, McKinley, I, 160; Muzzey, United States, II, 202; Nation, L (January 30, 1890), 81.

55. The minority report, submitted by Mills, objected to the numerous provisions in the bill calling for unprecedentedly high duties and criticized what was declared to be the assumption on the part of the Republicans that as industries became older they required increased protection. See McKinley, Tariff Legislation, 127-28.

56. Cong. Record, 51 Cong., 1 Sess., 4247-57 (May 7, 1890); Smith (comp.), Speeches of McKinley, 397-430.

57. Mills, in answering McKinley's speech, indicated disagreement with the latter's mandate idea and declared that "Grover Cleveland had a majority of 100,000 votes of the American people" in the election of 1888. Cong. Record, 51 Cong., 1 Sess., 4265 (May 7, 1890).

58. In a speech at Cleveland on October 6, 1889, McKinley had attributed to the protective tariff "the patriotic motive of taking care of our people." Smith (comp.), Speeches of McKinley, 372.

59. Olcott states that "While willing to admit that the Protective Tariff was not wholly responsible for the country's prosperity (though the fervor of his remarks sometimes indicates the contrary), McKinley was firmly convinced, that whatever may have been the effect of other causes, the prosperity could not have been achieved without the Protective System." Olcott, McKinley, I, 176.

60. See Peck, Twenty Years, 209.

61. The average rate of duty on raw sugar, nine-tenths of which was imported, had been two cents a pound. The sugar trust was further favored by the retention of a protective duty of a half-cent a pound on refined sugars, and a bounty of two cents a pound was granted domestic growers of sugar. Taussig, Tariff History, 276-77.

62. Peck, Twenty Years, 211. See also Tarbell, Nationalizing of Business, 196.

63. See Stanwood, Tariff Controversies, II, 268; Olcott, McKinley, I, 165-66.

64. The surplus revenue in 1889 had been slightly more than 105 million dollars and in the same year the receipts from sugar imports, constituting the most significant item in the customs collections, yielded almost 56 millions. See Noyes, American Finance, 134, 136; Taussig, Tariff History, 276; Olcott, McKinley, I, 164.

65. Stephenson, Aldrich, 83. See also Taussig, Tariff History, 278; Stanwood, Tariff Controversies, II, 266-67.

66. For McKinley's contemporary view that reciprocity agreements were detrimental to the United States, see Smith (comp.), Speeches of McKinley, 408. According to Olcott, McKinley had not given much attention to the subject of reciprocity in 1890, regarding the matter as being "more within the prov-

ince of the Department of State than in that of the Ways and Means Committee of the House." Olcott, McKinley, I, 179.

67. See Muzzey, Blaine, 449-50.

68. Ibid., 444.

69. For Blaine's activities in connection with the Pan-American Union, see Alice Felt Tyler, The Foreign Policy of James G. Blaine (Minneapolis, 1927), 46-106, 165-90; Muzzey, Blaine, 430-58; Thomas A. Bailey, A Diplomatic History of the American People (New York, 1950), 443-45; James W. Gantenbein (comp.), The Evolution of Our Latin-American Policy, A Documentary Record (New York, 1950), 54-58.

70. Stephenson, Aldrich, 83-84; Gail Hamilton (pseud., Mary Abigail Dodge), Biography of James G. Blaine (Norwich, Conn., 1895), 683-85; Muzzey, Blaine, 442-43; Peck, Twenty Years, 209-10.

71. See Hamilton, Blaine, 685.

72. The raw sugar duty, Muzzey notes, was the major asset on the part of the United States for securing reciprocity agreements. "With that we could bargain, offering its abolition in return for the free admission of our goods to Latin-American ports. But to remove the duty on sugar without exacting any quid pro quo from Cuba, Brazil or Venezuela was to throw away our one best chance of getting our due share of the Latin-American trade." Muzzey, Blaine, 443. Although Blaine's request for retention of the raw sugar duties as a phase of his reciprocity plan calling for the authorization of presidential efforts under the treaty power to secure mutual commercial concessions was rejected, his plea against the removal of hides from the free list was granted. See ibid., 444; Hamilton, Blaine, 682-83.

73. Stanwood, Tariff Controversies, II, 263.

74. Rhodes, History, VIII, 348.

75. See Stanwood, Tariff Controversies, II, 265; Tarbell, Nationalizing of Business, 198-99.

76. Stanwood, Tariff Controversies, II, 266. See also Rhodes, History, VIII, 348.

77. This feature of the tariff legislation of 1890 Tarbell describes as McKinley's personal victory, representing the outcome of a ten-year crusade for such a duty following his conversion to the idea at the hands of a steel-plate producer, W. C. Cronemeyer of Pittsburgh, who maintained that proper protection would assure the nation of an adequate supply of domestically manufactured tin plate. Tarbell, Nationalizing of Business, 197-98. See also Tarbell, Tariff, 190-92.

78. Tarbell, Nationalizing of Business, 197.

79. Stanwood, Tariff Controversies, II, 264.

80. Ibid., 273.

81. Olcott notes that the McKinley bill was approved by the House on May 21 "by a vote of 164 yeas, all Republicans, and 142 nays, all Democrats but two,—one Republican and one Independent. Six Republicans and fifteen Democrats did not vote." Olcott, McKinley, I, 177. See also McKinley, Tariff Legislation, 139; Cong. Record, 51 Cong., 1 Sess., 5112-13 (May 21, 1890); Public Opinion, IX (May 31, 1890), 165.

82. See Robinson, Reed, 242-43; Paxson, op. cit., XII, 106.

83. According to Robinson, Reed "admitted that in some of the schedules protection had been carried to an extreme." Robinson, Reed, 241. McKinley when asked why he had consented to some of the very high duties replied that he had done so to facilitate passage of the bill. "I realized," he asserted, "that some things were too high, but I couldn't get my bill

through without it." Quoted in Olcott, McKinley, I, 127.

84. Robinson, Reed, 241. See also Peck, Twenty Years, 213.

85. Ibid., 213.

86. Reed was reported to have described the Senate as a gathering of "'tabby cats'" and "'old grannies,'" and as "'a place where good Representatives went when they died.'" He objected to the indulgence on the part of dignified solons in time-consuming oratory. Robinson, Reed, 77, 240.

87. Stephenson, Aldrich, 88-90, 163. In order to preserve the vitality of the tariff measure, Aldrich, a gold advocate, supported the movement for the enactment of the compromise silver purchase bill. When he failed in his effort to invoke cloture so as to secure an early vote on the tariff bill, he joined in the acceptance of a Quay-sponsored compromise proposal. This cleared the way for the passage of the tariff measure by postponing until the following session the consideration of the House-approved Federal Election bill, thus dissolving a legislation-blocking combination of Southerners and Western silverites. See George F. Hoar, Autobiography of Seventy Years (2 vols., New York, 1903), II, 150-56; Stephenson, Aldrich, 89 and note 19, 438; Cullom, Fifty Years, 255; Muzzey, United States, II, 206-208; Franklin L. Burdette, Filibustering in the Senate (Princeton, 1940), 52.

88. In a letter of June 4, 1890 transmitting to the President an International American Conference report recommending a customs union, Blaine brought his reciprocity suggestions directly to the attention of Harrison, who responded favorably by sending the recommendations to Congress on June 19. Stanwood, Tariff Controversies, II, 276-77; Cong. Record, 51 Cong., 1 Sess., 6256-59 (June 19, 1890); McKinley,

Tariff Legislation, 141; Richardson (ed.), Messages, IX, 74. According to Hamilton, Blaine in an appearance before the Senate Finance Committee expressed his anger with the reciprocity-lacking tariff measure by striking his fist against the bill, crushing his hat, and branding the removal of the duty on sugar as "the most inexcusable piece of folly" ever committed by his party. He further declared: "'Pass this bill, and in 1892 there will not be a man in all the party so beggared as to accept your nomination for the presidency.'" Hamilton, Blaine, 685. See also Muzzey, Blaine, 444-45; Stephenson, Aldrich, 84. Dunn states that Blaine gave rein to his anger before the Finance Committee "because such men as Morrill, Aldrich, Sherman, and Allison could not appreciate the glories of reciprocity." Dunn, Harrison to Harding, I, 44.

89. Stephenson, Aldrich, 87.

90. See ibid., 85.

91. See ibid., 87.

92. Muzzey observes that Blaine's advocacy of reciprocity "had a tremendous effect on the people of the West, who saw in it the promise of enlarged markets for their produce. . . . Indeed, the effect of the tariff bill on the West was a prime concern of the protectionist leaders." Muzzey, Blaine, 447. See also Taussig, Tariff History, 278.

93. Cong. Record, 51 Cong., 1 Sess., 9250 (August 28, 1890); Stephenson, Aldrich, note 13, 437.

94. Muzzey, Blaine, 448.

95. See Stephenson, Aldrich, 87-88.

96. Muzzey, Blaine, 449; Tarbell, Tariff, 206.

97. Blaine's recommendations were embodied in the Hale amendment, which was introduced on June 19. See Stanwood, Tariff Controversies, II, 277; Muzzey,

Blaine, 448-50; Cong. Record, 51 Cong., 1 Sess., 6259 (June 19, 1890).

98. Josephson, Politicos, 454.

99. Even the restricted Aldrich reciprocity provision was criticized as an unconstitutional delegation of the taxing power to the executive. This view was expressed by Democrats and by the New York Republican, Senator Evarts, who was supported in his opposition to the amendment by Senator Edmunds of Vermont. Stanwood, Tariff Controversies, II, 282; Tarbell, Tariff, 206. See also Public Opinion, IX (September 6, 1890), 497 (September 20, 1890), 543.

100. The vote consisted of 40 Republican yeas and 29 Democratic nays. Cong. Record, 51 Cong., 1 Sess., 9943 (September 10, 1890); McKinley, Tariff Legislation, 142; Nation, LI (September 18, 1890), 219, (September 25, 1890), 238.

101. In the House the vote was 151 to 81, and in the Senate, 33 to 27. See Cong. Record, 51 Cong., 1 Sess., 10641 (September 27, 1890), 10740 (September 30, 1890); McKinley, Tariff Legislation, 143; Olcott, McKinley, I, 179; Oberholtzer, History, V, 111; Public Opinion, IX (September 20, 1890), 543-56, (September 27, 1890), 567-68. For detailed provisions of the tariff act of 1890, see Statutes at Large of the United States of America, XXVI (1889-1891), 567-625.

102. Cong. Record, 51 Cong., 1 Sess., 6207 (June 18, 1890). See also George H. Haynes, The Senate of the United States: Its History and Practice (2 vols., Boston, 1938), I, 442.

103. Stanwood, Tariff Controversies, II, 263. The profound modification of the act in the upper chamber, Stanwood states, "is made clear by the fact that that body made 496 amendments to the bill as passed by the House. It ultimately receded from only 51 of

these amendments; the House accepted 272 of them without change; and the two branches of Congress compromised upon the other 173." Ibid., 263. See also McKinley, Tariff Legislation, 142.

104. Tarbell, Tariff, 206.

105. McKinley, Tariff Legislation, 143. See also Olcott, McKinley, I, 179.

106. Tarbell, Tariff, 206-208.

107. Ibid., 207. Cullom states that the McKinley act "was a high protective tariff, dictated by the manufacturers of the country." Cullom, Fifty Years, 253.

108. Tarbell, Tariff, 207.

109. See ibid., 207-208. Barry states that Aldrich "regarded speech-making of the ordinary kind as just the blowing off of so much froth." Barry, Forty Years, 157.

110. Ibid., 152. Although Barry observes that "It has been said by contemporaries of the Rhode Island Senator that he had more concrete and natural ability than any man who has appeared in Congress in half a century," less laudatory appraisals are presented by Steffens and Needham. Ibid., 153; Lincoln Steffens, The Autobiography of Lincoln Steffens (New York, 1931), 504; Needham, op. cit., XI, 7064-65.

111. Steffens, op. cit., XXIV, 337.

112. Ibid., 337.

113. John Chamberlain, Farewell to Reform: The Rise, Life and Decay of the Progressive Mind in America (2d ed., New York, 1933), 41. In regard to Aldrich's subservience to Morgan, see Steffens, Autobiography, 506. "In 1901," Phillips notes, Aldrich's "daughter married the only son and destined successor of John D. Rockefeller." Phillips, op. cit., XL, 631. See also Steffens, op. cit., XXIV, 337; Stephenson, Aldrich, 173; Chamberlain, Farewell to Reform, 139.

114. See Stephenson, "Aldrich," Dictionary of American Biography, I, 152, 153.

115. See Stephenson, Aldrich, 60.

116. Tarbell, Tariff, 207.

117. Aldrich defended the preferential treatment of manufacturers over farmers by maintaining "that even the agricultural interest would be better served by an abundance of American labor and by busy factories and teeming markets than by legislation supposed to be more directly for its own good." Stephenson, Aldrich, 80-81. Unlike McKinley, Aldrich did not hedge regarding the charge that the tariff was aimed at increasing consumer prices; he flatly stated that without such price rises protectionist legislation would have no effect or force. Cong. Record, 51 Cong., 1 Sess., 4123 (May 2, 1890); Stephenson, Aldrich, note 8, 436. McKinley displayed less ingenuousness. See his remarks at Cleveland, October 6, 1889, in Smith (comp.), Speeches of McKinley, 372. See also ibid., 294; Rhodes, History, VIII, 349; Olcott, McKinley, I, 162-63.

118. Tarbell, Nationalizing of Business, 195. See also Shannon, Economic History, 580.

119. Muzzey, United States, II, 211.

120. Noyes cites as 48.71 per cent the average level of rates established by the McKinley act as compared with the previous level of 44.41 per cent. Noyes, American Finance, 134. Shannon states that the average rate under the act of 1890 was 49.5 per cent. Shannon, Economic History, 580.

121. See ibid., 580.

122. Ibid., 579; Muzzey, United States, II, 211. See also Olcott, McKinley, I, 179; Dewey, Financial History, 438; Tarbell, Tariff, 206.

123. McKinley had declared in his May 7 House speech that the Ways and Means Committee had "not been compelled to abolish the internal-revenue system that we might preserve the protective system, which we were pledged to do in the event the abolition of the one was essential to the preservation of the other." Cong. Record, 51 Cong., 1 Sess., 4247 (May 7, 1890); Smith (comp.), Speeches of McKinley, 398.

124. Peck, Twenty Years, 212-13. See also Stanwood, Tariff Controversies, II, 288-94; Muzzey, United States, II, 211; Olcott, McKinley, I, 180; Shannon, Economic History, 581-82.

125. Although the act was approved by the President on October 1, 1890, the sugar provisions were to remain inoperative until April 1, 1891, thus withholding for a six-month period the "great boon of free sugar." Stanwood, Tariff Controversies, II, 287. As a result of this delay the Republican campaign slogan of the "free breakfast table," referring to the inclusion of coffee, tea, and sugar in the free list, could hardly prove effective. See Rhodes, History, VIII, 366.

126. Muzzey, Blaine, 454-55. See also Taussig, Tariff History, 284; Rhodes, History, VIII, 365; Cullom, Fifty Years, 258; Tarbell, Tariff, 210; Stanwood, Tariff Controversies, II, 294. Also reflected in the election were such factors as disapproval of Reed's tyranny in the House and dissatisfaction with the methods employed by the Republicans in securing the enactment of their legislative program. See Muzzey, United States, II, 212-13; Taussig, Tariff History, 285; Tarbell, Tariff, 210.

127. In the crushing Republican defeat of 1890, even such supposedly Republican states as Massachusetts, Illinois, Ohio, and Michigan sent majorities of Democrats to Congress, as did also Wisconsin, Iowa, and Kansas. In the Senate the Republicans retained a

majority whose margin of only eight members included silverites from Nevada, Wyoming, Washington, Idaho, Montana, and North Dakota. See
Josephson, Politicos, 464; Oberholtzer, History, V,
136; Tarbell, Tariff, 210; Olcott, McKinley, I, 181;
Peck, Twenty Years, 214; Morison and Commager,
American Republic, II, 235; Stanwood, Tariff Controversies, II, 294-95; Taussig, Tariff History, 284;
Muzzey, Blaine, 455; Rhodes, History, VIII, 366-67;
Public Opinion, X (November 8, 1890), 99, (November 15, 1890), 123.

128. Rhodes notes that although McKinley's defeat "was
due to a gerrymander by a Democratic legislature
which took his county out of a reasonably certain
Republican district," his attempt would nevertheless
have been successful if the tariff act had proved
popular. Rhodes, History, VIII, 367.

129. Many of the importers who participated in this conspiracy, McKinley declared, "were not even citizens
of the United States." He also asserted that "the
people who have been duped will not forget. Nor
will the friends of protection lower their flag or
raise the British flag." Quoted in Olcott, McKinley,
I, 187. Olcott and Stanwood stress the detrimental
effects upon Republican efforts of the "misrepre-
sentation" and "exaggeration" regarding price-
raising effects of the McKinley act. See ibid., I,
180-81; Stanwood, Tariff Controversies, II, 290,
292-95.

130. Robinson, Reed, 241; Peck, Twenty Years, note 38,
215-16. See also Thomas B. Reed, "Historic Political Upheavals," North American Review, CLX
(January, 1895), 113-14.

131. Stephenson, Aldrich, 90-91.

132. "Tin plates which sold for $4.79 a box in 1890 sold
for $5.33 in 1891, and by the time the tin found its

way into a milk pan or a dinner pail or a tomato can there was a still greater per cent of increase. It was so palpably a higher cost because of the duty, it was so generally and correctly believed that the increase would not for many years benefit more than a few, that irritation increased with every purchase." Tarbell, Tariff, 211.

133. Cullom, Fifty Years, 257-58.

134. The Democrats, in addition to carrying the South, retained the support of such states as Illinois, Indiana, and Wisconsin and were likewise successful in the presumably doubtful Eastern states of New York, Connecticut, and New Jersey. The attainment of a Senate majority by the Democrats in 1892 constituted their first realization of that objective since the term from 1879 to 1881 and their last until 1913. See Muzzey, United States, II, 246; Taussig, Tariff History, 284-85; Cullom, Fifty Years, 258.

1. See Josephson, Politicos, 638.

2. Sherman, who had been jarred by Cleveland's call for
tariff reduction in his annual message of December 6,
1887, regarded the President's tariff remarks in his
second inaugural address as sufficiently vague to permit agreement on the part of protectionists. Sherman, Recollections, II, 1004-1005, 1181. See also
Cullom, Fifty Years, 264; Richardson (ed.), Messages, IX, 458-60. That Cleveland's views were not
in accord with the Democratic tariff plank of 1892,
which, forced upon him against his will, denounced
"Republican protection as a fraud, a robbery of the
great majority of the people for the benefit of the few,"
and characterized the law of 1890 "as the culminating
atrocity of class legislation," appears clear from the
temperate remarks in his acceptance letter of 1892.
His party, he had stated, waged "no exterminating
war against any American interests," and he had expressed the belief that readjustment of the tariff could
"be accomplished . . . without disaster or demolition."
Quoted in Tarbell, Tariff, 215. See also Public
Opinion, XIII (October 1, 1892), 613; "Mr. Cleveland's
Letter of Acceptance," Harper's Weekly, XXXVI (October 8, 1892), 962. Josephson observes that Cleveland in his quest for tariff reduction "exercised no
such iron leadership as he demonstrated in the earlier
struggle for silver repeal." Josephson, Politicos,
550. See also ibid., 498; Porter (comp.), Party Platforms, 160, 161; McKee (ed.), Conventions and Platforms, 263.

3. See Cullom, Fifty Years, 264; Oberholtzer, History, V, 274-75; Tarbell, Tariff, 217; Shannon, Economic History, 584.

4. Noyes, in pointing out that tariff legislation would have been necessary regardless of which party had been in power, states that "the existing revenue law had proved its inability, under prevailing trade conditions, to meet the expenses of Government." The deficit in revenue, he adds, "had been continuous in every quarter since September, 1892, and had amounted in the five months ending with November, 1893, to nearly thirty million dollars." Noyes, American Finance, 222, 223.

5. In the adoption of this approach the Republicans were fulfilling Cleveland's expectation that Democratic purposes would be misrepresented. See Tarbell, Tariff, 215-16.

6. Whereas the large Democratic House majority impaired the sense of individual responsibility, the slender Democratic majority in the Senate endangered the maintenance of legislative control. It was in Cleveland's relations with the upper chamber that his notorious inability to work smoothly with Congress became especially apparent. Irritated by his domineering insistence upon the repeal of the silver purchase act, many solons regarded him with hostility. In their attitude was reflected not only bitterness carried over from quarrels during his first term but also what Peck describes as "the traditional antagonism which most Senators entertain toward every President who has not had congressional experience sufficient to make him understand and properly respect the usages, the prerogatives and the prejudices of the senatorial body." Peck, Twenty Years, 359. See also Dewey, National Problems, 277; Taussig, Tariff History, 287; Josephson, Politicos, 530-31, 536; Rhodes, History, VIII, 458-59.

7. The measure, entitled "A bill to reduce taxation, to provide revenue for the Government, and for other purposes," was formulated in the House under the supervision of chairman James L. Wilson of the Ways and Means Committee, and thus came to be known as the Wilson bill. It was reported to the House on December 19, 1893, and was subjected to debate on January 9, 1894. Cong. Record, 53 Cong., 2 Sess., 415 (December 19, 1893), 572 (January 9, 1894). See also Taussig, Tariff History, 288-89.

8. Republican criticisms of the Ways and Means Committee Stanwood characterizes as "political only." Stanwood, Tariff Controversies, II, 319. See also Kerr, Sherman, II, 335.

9. The bill was passed without Republican support, the vote being 204 to 140. Stanwood, Tariff Controversies, II, 326; Cong. Record, 53 Cong., 2 Sess., 1796 (February 1, 1894); Kerr, Sherman, II, 334.

10. See Tarbell, Tariff, 218-20. According to Josephson, the Wilson bill, "by the timidity of its measures, provided a shock for all true tariff-reformers." Josephson, Politicos, 543.

11. Taussig, Tariff History, 289.

12. Peck, Twenty Years, 356, 358.

13. James A. Barnes, John G. Carlisle, Financial Statesman (New York, 1931), 304; Muzzey, United States, II, 255.

14. Intended to decrease protection while providing for greater revenue, the measure added wool, flax, hemp, iron ore, coal, lumber, and refined sugar to the free list. With the purpose of extending aid to agriculture, duties were removed from farm machinery, cotton bagging, salt, and binding twine. Moderately reduced rates were applied to pig iron, steel rails, tin plate, china-ware, glass, cottons, silks, linens, and woolens.

Provision was made for the replacement, when prac-
ticable, of ad valorem by specific duties. Moreover,
the bill slightly increased such internal revenue rates
as those on tobacco, liquors, and playing cards.
Dewey, National Problems, 281; Tarbell, Tariff, 218;
Shannon, Economic History, 583; Peck, Twenty Years,
356-58; Muzzey, United States, II, 254.

15. Stanwood, Tariff Controversies, II, 324; Josephson,
Politicos, 554; Peck, Twenty Years, 359; Charles
Manfred Thompson and Fred Mitchell Jones, Economic
Development of the United States (New York, 1939),
308.

16. William Withers, Public Finance (New York, 1948), 45.

17. James A. Maxwell, The Fiscal Impact of Federalism
in the United States (Cambridge, 1946), 22. See also
Robinson, Reed, 304; Barnes, Carlisle, 324. Designed
partly to secure agrarian Democratic and Populistic
support for the tariff measure and partly to offset the
anticipated $50,000,000 loss of revenue from rate re-
ductions, the income tax amendment was introduced
in the House on January 29, 1894 by Representative
McMillan of Tennessee. Although not included in the
Democratic platform of 1892, the demand for an income tax had appeared in the Populist Omaha platform of that year. Advocates of the tax regarded it
as a means of more equitably distributing the financial burdens of the government. See Cong. Record.
53 Cong., 2 Sess., 1594 (January 29, 1894); Stanwood,
Tariff Controversies, II, 324; Dewey, National Problems, 281-82; Peck, Twenty Years, 358-59; Kerr,
Sherman, II, 333-34.

18. Cullom, Fifty Years, 268.

19. The income tax amendment was adopted in the lower
chamber by a vote of 182 to 48, with 122 Representatives not participating. Cong. Record, 53 Cong., 2
Sess., 1795-96 (February 1, 1894); Stanwood, Tariff
Controversies, II, 325.

20. Barnes, Carlisle, 323-24.

21. Cong. Record, 53 Cong., 2 Sess., 1781-88 (February 1, 1894). See also Robinson, Reed, 306-10; McCall, Reed, 199-205.

22. Josephson, Politicos, 545.

23. Peck, Twenty Years, 359. Tarbell observes that in the Senate "the industrial interests of the nation had a stronger proportionate representation" than in the House. Tarbell, Nationalizing of Business, 200. Illustrative of the manner in which the minority party was aided by the exertion of industrialist influence upon majority Senators was the close relationship between the Republican, Carnegie, and the Maryland Democrat, Arthur P. Gorman. So intimate were their relations that in compliance with Gorman's invitation the wealthy manufacturer gave his assistance in the drafting of the iron and steel schedules. Carnegie gave Gorman major credit for revising the tariff bill in accord with protectionist principles. Andrew Carnegie, "My Experience with, and Views upon, the Tariff," Century Magazine (New York), New Series, LV (December, 1908), 199. See also Rhodes, History, VIII, 419-20.

24. Peck, Twenty Years, 360. Ford calls attention to "the habitual disposition of the Senate, when dealing with business interests, to decide questions by private conference and personal agreements, while maintaining a surface show of party controversy." Ford, Cleveland Era, 197. See also Phillips, "The Treason of the Senate," Cosmopolitan Magazine, XLI (May, 1906), 4, 9-12; Needham, op. cit., XI, 7061.

25. Also of significance in giving a highly protectionist cast to the Senate measure was the desire of Democrats to secure protection which would be applicable in their own states. Cullom, Fifty Years, 265-66. See also Frederick H. Gillett, George Frisbie Hoar (Boston and New York, 1934), 157.

26. Aldrich and Gorman, Stephenson observes, "were good cronies in private, even business associates." Stephenson, Aldrich, 105. See also ibid., 109; Phillips, op. cit., XL, 633; XLI, 9, 12; Needham, op. cit., XI, 7211.

27. Haynes, Senate, I, 444.

28. Josephson, Politicos, 544.

29. See Rhodes, History, VIII, 420; Tarbell, Tariff, 221; Stanwood, Tariff Controversies, II, 326-27; Phillips, op. cit., XL, 635; XLI, 10.

30. Edward Stanwood, A History of the Presidency (2 vols., new ed., New York, 1928), I, 524.

31. Stanwood, Tariff Controversies, II, 334-35; Cong. Record, 53 Cong., 2 Sess., 4665 (May 12, 1894).

32. Stephenson, Aldrich, 112.

33. Ibid., 117. Earlier, as Stanwood observes, Aldrich had "lost no occasion to taunt his political opponents upon their plight, owing to their ignorance of the extent of the concessions that would be required." Stanwood, Tariff Controversies, II, 332.

34. Stephenson, Aldrich, 117.

35. Ibid., 116.

36. Although a number of Senators, including Sherman, Hoar, and Aldrich were subjected to questioning, only two of them, J. R. McPherson of New Jersey and Quay of Pennsylvania admitted the accusation. Quay declared that his speculating activities had not been confined to sugar, and he felt that his membership in the Senate should in no way restrict his freedom as a purchaser of stocks. Tarbell, Nationalizing of Business, 201; Stephenson, Aldrich, 120; Josephson, Politicos, 549. Despite denials, there remained widespread suspicion that other solons were similarly guilty, and this belief, Tarbell observes, was intrenched most strongly around Aldrich. Tarbell,

Tariff, 227. Although the investigation was to deal also with charges that pressure from the sugar trust had resulted in the acceptance of bribes by Senators, this phase of the inquiry was not pursued. It was during this investigation that H. O. Havemeyer, head of the sugar trust, denied any special attachment to either of the major parties, while acknowledging that his firm engaged in what he regarded as the common practice of making financial contributions to both political parties with a view toward securing favors from whichever side might be successful in elections. See ibid., 226; Josephson, Politicos, 548-49; Taussig, Tariff History, 314; Henry Jones Ford, The Cleveland Era: A Chronicle of the New Order in Politics, Vol. XLIV of The Chronicles of America Series (New Haven, 1921), 201. See also Phillips, op. cit., XL, 635; XLI, 11; Public Opinion, XVII (August 9, 1894), 437-38. The sugar scandal, according to Dewey, "permanently injured the reputation of the Senate." Dewey, National Problems, 284.

37. Stephenson, Aldrich, 116.

38. Tarbell, Tariff, 228-29. See also Barnes, Carlisle, 339.

39. Democratic Senator David B. Hill of New York branded the proposal as sectional, inquisitorial, and socialistic. It was intended, he charged, to draw from the wealthy the money for operating the government. See Cong. Record, 53 Cong., 2 Sess., 3558-66 (April 9, 1894), 6764-70 (June 23, 1894), 6865-66 (June 27, 1894); Kerr, Sherman, II, 337; Public Opinion, XVII (June 28, 1894), 281, 282, (July 12, 1894), 335.

40. Pollock v. Farmers' Loan and Trust Co., 157 U.S. 429 (1895) and 158 U.S. 601 (1895). See also Clarence A. Stern, Republican Heyday: Republicanism Through the McKinley Years (Ann Arbor, 1969), 19-20.

41. Stephenson, Aldrich, 113.

42. As Stephenson observes, Aldrich "expressed the view of the creditor class of that day, severely disapproving an income tax." Ibid., 113. See also ibid., 126, 127; Cong. Record, 53 Cong., 2 Sess., 6867, 6876, 6880, 6893 (June 27, 1894). In regard to Allison's co-operation with Aldrich in opposing the income tax, see Phillips, op. cit., XL, 637. Concerning the objections of Sherman, O. H. Platt, and Cullom to the income tax amendment, see Cong. Record, 53 Cong., 2 Sess., 6694-96, 6701-6706 (June 22, 1894), 6874-75 (June 27, 1894); Theodore E. Burton, John Sherman (Boston and New York, 1906), 393; Louis A. Coolidge, An Old-Fashioned Senator, Orville H. Platt (New York, 1910), 450-54; Cullom, Fifty Years, 268.

43. See Cong. Record, 53 Cong., 2 Sess., 5505-20 (May 31, 1894). See also Sherman, Recollections, II, 1202-1207; Kerr, Sherman, II, 339-40; Burton, Sherman, 392; Ford, Cleveland Era, 199.

44. Sherman, Recollections, II, 1205.

45. Ibid., 1203.

46. Stanwood, Tariff Controversies, II, 335-36. Hides were retained on the free list. Also duty-free were binding twine, cotton ties, and fresh fish. Rhodes, History, VIII, 422. Stanwood states that "It would be absurd, and no Democrat ever attempted, to represent the bill, as the Senate framed it and as it became law, as a 'lightening of the burdens of taxation upon the people' in the sense given to that phrase prior to the meeting of Congress." Stanwood, Tariff Controversies, II, 336. The bill passed the Senate by a vote of 39 to 34. Cong. Record, 53 Cong., 2 Sess., 7136 (July 3, 1894). For complete statement of the Wilson-Gorman act see Statutes at Large, XXVIII, 509-70.

47. "The final outcome," Taussig states, "was more than satisfactory to the Sugar Trust." Taussig, Tariff

History, 313. See also ibid., 312, 314; Josephson, Politicos, 545, 547-48; Tarbell, Tariff, 226-27; Stephenson, Aldrich, 119-20; Shannon, Economic History, 583-84.

48. Democratic discord was aggravated by Cleveland's futile attempt to secure the modification of the Senate-approved tariff bill along the lines of avowed party principles. Such revision he appears to have sought by encouraging the House to persist in disagreement with the upper chamber until some concessions were made. In accord with this purpose, Wilson on July 19 had the clerk read into the Record a letter from Cleveland expressing dissatisfaction with the Senate bill, declaring that abandonment of Democratic tariff principles meant "party perfidy and party dishonor," and intimating that the sugar trust had played a part in the determination of duties on sugar. "From a party point of view," Peck states in connection with this letter, "a Democratic President was arraigning Democratic Senators before both Democratic and Republican Representatives." In retaliation against the President, Gorman in a Senate speech on July 23 challenged Cleveland's veracity by indicating that his approval of the amendments had been gained prior to the passage of the bill by the upper chamber. See Cong. Record, 53 Cong., 2 Sess., 7189-96 (July 7, 1894); Cleveland to Wilson, July 2, 1894, ibid., 7712-13 (July 19, 1894), 7803-7809 (July 23, 1894); McKinley, Tariff Legislation, 222-24; Barry, Forty Years, 194-97; Tarbell, Tariff, 230-34; Stanwood, Tariff Controversies, II, 345; Peck, Twenty Years, 365-67; Ford, Cleveland Era, 198; Dewey, National Problems, 285; Barnes, Carlisle, 339.

49. Cong. Record, 53 Cong., 2 Sess., 7191 (July 7, 1894).

50. Ibid., 7192.

51. Ibid., 7710, 7713 (July 19, 1894).

52. As a result of the inflexible attitude of the Gorman
    bloc of Senators, the Democratic House leaders re-
    ceded from their earlier position after making a futile
    attempt to secure a face-saving compromise calling
    for slightly modified duties on sugar. Fearful that the
    Senate was prepared to terminate the conference and
    thus prevent the enactment of a tariff measure, the
    Democratic House yielded unconditionally. Ineffective
    was its effort to mitigate its humiliation by passing
    bills, never voted upon by the upper chamber, pro-
    viding for the elimination of duties on iron ore, coal,
    barbed wire, and sugar. See Stanwood, Tariff Con-
    troversies, II, 351-52; Robinson, Reed, 312; McCall,
    Reed, 207; Dewey, National Problems, 286; Ford,
    Cleveland Era, 198-99. See also Public Opinion, XVII
    (August 16, 1894), 461-62, (August 23, 1894), 485-88,
    (August 30, 1894), 511-13. By Brown the capitulation
    of the House is characterized as "an abject surrender"
    to the oligarchic upper chamber, and Haynes refers to
    the development as a "striking illustration of Senate
    domination in tariff-making." Brown, Leadership of
    Congress, 104; Haynes, Senate, I, 442.

53. Cong. Record, 53 Cong., 2 Sess., 8470-71 (August 13,
    1894).

54. Cleveland chose to permit the measure to become law
    without his signature. In a letter to Representative
    Thomas C. Catchings of Mississippi, Cleveland ex-
    plained that despite his disappointment with the legis-
    lation he preferred to avoid such separation from the
    Democratic party as a veto might imply. Although
    "the livery of Democratic reform" had, in his opinion,
    "been stolen and worn in the service of Republican
    protection," he maintained that the act of 1894 repre-
    sented an improvement over existing tariff legislation.
    See Cleveland to Catchings, August 27, 1894, Public
    Opinion, XVII (August 30, 1894), 511-12; McKinley,
    Tariff Legislation, 229-31; Cullom, Fifty Years, 268;
    Stanwood, Tariff Controversies, II, 354. According to

Peck, Cleveland was "ashamed to sign" the tariff act of 1894. Peck, Twenty Years, 405. See also Shannon, Economic History, 584.

55. This year, referred to by Barnes as calamitous for the Democrats, witnessed not only the growth of party discord but also the continuation of the economic depression and the development of labor unrest characterized by violent strikes. Barnes, Carlisle, 361; Holcombe, Political Parties, 233; Peck, Twenty Years, 405-406; James Albert Woodburn, Political Parties and Party Problems in the United States: A Sketch of American Party History and of the Development and Operations of Party Machinery, Together with a Consideration of Certain Party Problems in Their Relations to Political Morality (New York, 1909), 125.

56. Holcombe, Political Parties, 233. See also Stanwood, Tariff Controversies, II, 525.

57. Croly, Hanna, 172. In connection with the Republican practice of blaming the Wilson-Gorman law for the continuation of the depressed condition of the economy, Shannon observes that "By election time it was even being asserted that the tariff act had caused the Panic of 1893. If corrected as to chronology, politicians could still say that fear of a Democratic tariff had caused the panic, while the act itself had added to hard times." Shannon, Economic History, 584.

58. In accord with Reed's prediction of an impressive victory for the Republicans, they secured 245 House seats as against only 104 for the Democrats. In the Senate the Republican strength increased from a membership of 36 to 43 in a chamber including 39 Democrats and 6 Populists. See Robinson, Reed, 321, 322; Barnes, Carlisle, 353; Peck, Twenty Years, 406; Ford, Cleveland Era, 217; McKinley, Tariff Legislation, 232.

59. See Croly, Hanna, 172-73. In Croly's view the unsuccessful Democratic attempt at tariff revision had the

effect of making McKinley "the logical [presidential] candidate of his own party" in the campaign of 1896. Ibid., 167. For McKinley's view of the election of 1894 as constituting an overwhelming endorsement of the protectionist doctrine, see McKinley, Tariff Legislation, 231-32.

60. Stanwood, History of Presidency, I, 525; Peck, Twenty Years, 406.

61. Robinson, Reed, 324; Burton, Sherman, 395.

62. Robinson, Reed, 324.

63. Ibid., 324-26. See also Oberholtzer, History, V, 382.

64. See Josephson, Politicos, 637-38; Barnes, Carlisle, 312; Kerr, Sherman, II, 343-44; Appletons' Cyclopaedia, 3d s., I (1896), 183; Barnes, Carlisle, 317, 452.

65. Cleveland's insistence upon the redemption of the silver notes in gold led to the implementation, between January, 1894 and January, 1896, of four bond issues. The first two issues of $50,000,000 each had failed to protect the gold reserve from the depletory effects of the gold withdrawal practices characterizing the "endless chain." The third issue, made in February, 1895, took the form of the so-called Morgan-Belmont contract. Under this agreement, which brought in about $65,000,000 in gold at a time when the gold reserve had dwindled to approximately $41,000,000, the bankers arranged for the importation of 50 per cent of the gold and promised to apply their efforts to prevent gold withdrawals for a half-year period. Still in need of bolstering following this contract under which, according to Shannon, the bankers "made an immediate profit of at least $7,000,000 without effort," the reserve received an additional $100,000,000 in gold as the result of a bond issue in January, 1896. Despite a temporary continuation of gold withdrawals, further issues were unnecessary. See ibid., 286; Coolidge,

O. H. Platt, 186; Noyes, American Finance, 207-53;
Josephson, Politicos, 540, 590-603, 626-29; Shannon,
Economic History, 482-83. See also Reginald C.
McGrane, The Economic Development of the American
Nation (Boston, 1942), 452; Frederick Lewis Allen,
The Great Pierpont Morgan (New York, 1949), 99-125;
Lewis Corey, The House of Morgan: A Social Biog-
raphy of the Masters of Money (New York, 1930), 183-
91; Herbert L. Satterlee, J. Pierpont Morgan: An
Intimate Portrait (New York, 1939), 279-99; Carl
Hovey, The Life Story of J. Pierpont Morgan: A
Biography (New York, 1911), 176-92.

66. Highlighted by Bryan's declaration, during his de-
nunciation of the Morgan-Belmont contract, that the
Democrats had undergone "blood poisoning" by a
President determined to inject "Republican virus"
into his own party, the Democratic sectional breach
became progressively worse. Bryan deplored the
divisive effect of the Eastern demands for hard money,
and he asserted that on questions of finance Eastern
Republicans locked arms with Eastern Democrats.
This example of sectionalism, he warned, would in
time force the West and South to protect their interests through unified action. Cong. Record, 53 Cong.,
3 Sess., Appendix, 285, 287 (February 14, 1895);
William J. Bryan, The First Battle: A Story of the
Campaign of 1896 (Chicago, 1896), 136, 146. See also
Barnes, Carlisle, 390, 436; Robinson, Reed, 319;
Oberholtzer, History, V, 311-12; Ford, Cleveland Era,
214; Woodburn, Political Parties, 124-25.

67. See Dunn, Harrison to Harding, I, 160; Josephson,
Politicos, 638.

68. This bill, characterized by Oberholtzer as "a mere
campaign document," was approved by the lower
chamber on December 26, 1895 but was impeded by
the silverites in the Senate. Oberholtzer, History, V,
381; Cong. Record, 54 Cong., 1 Sess., 326-27 (December 26, 1895).

NOTES - THE DINGLEY TARIFF

1. See James Ford Rhodes, The McKinley and Roosevelt Administrations, 1897-1909 (New York, 1922), 36.

2. Stanwood observes that those favoring priority for tariff revision argued that "so long as the Republicans were in control of the administration there was no danger whatever that the country would be allowed to fall to a silver basis." Stanwood, Tariff Controversies, II, 377-78. See also Clarence A. Stern, Golden Republicanism: The Crusade for Hard Money (Ann Arbor, 1970), 54-55.

3. Croly, Hanna, 274-75.

4. See Noyes, American Finance, 269. According to Ashley, McKinley "could scarcely claim that the nation had given a definite judgment on the tariff problem," and Shannon states that the Republican victory "did not signify that the people wanted a change in tariff policy." Both of these authorities call attention to the decrease in the treasury deficit under the operation of the Wilson-Gorman act, involving a reduction from $70,000,000 for the fiscal year of 1893-1894 to $18,000,000 for that of 1896-1897. Ashley, Tariff History, 219; Shannon, Economic History, 585. See also Harold U. Faulkner, The Decline of Laissez Faire, 1897-1917, Vol. VII of The Economic History of the United States (New York, 1951), 59. In the platform of 1896 the Republicans reiterated their "allegiance to the policy of protection as the bulwark of American industrial independence and the foundation of American development and prosperity." "In its reasonable application" this "true American policy" was described as being "just, fair, and impartial;

equally opposed to foreign control and domestic monopoly, to sectional discrimination and individual favoritism." The Wilson-Gorman tariff was characterized as "sectional, injurious to the public credit, and destructive to business enterprise." In place of that legislation was demanded "such an equitable tariff on foreign imports which come into competition with American products as will not only furnish adequate revenue for the necessary expenses of the government, but will protect American labor from degradation to the wage level of other lands." McKee (ed.), Conventions and Platforms, 300-301; Porter (comp.), Party Platforms, 202-203.

5. Peck, Twenty Years, 524.

6. Tarbell, Tariff, 241. See also Coolidge, O. H. Platt, 255; Paxson, op. cit., XII, 107.

7. Peck, Twenty Years, 524. Taussig observes that the methods employed in the preparation of the tariff bill "paid scant respect to the letter of the law" and adds that "Strictly, so long as the new Congress had not met, no one was authorized to take any steps towards legislation at its hands." Taussig, Tariff History, 326.

8. Rhodes, McKinley and Roosevelt Administrations, 37; Oberholtzer, History, V, 459; Coolidge, O. H. Platt, 252-53; Stanwood, History of Presidency, II, 4; E. N. Dingley, Dingley, 417-20; "Tariff-Making Extraordinary," Nation, LXIV (April 8, 1897), 256.

9. Stanwood, History of Presidency, II, 4.

10. E. N. Dingley, Dingley, 423.

11. Ibid., 424. Tarbell states that Dingley, whose devotion to the protective system was as strong as McKinley's, "probably knew more about tariff schedules than any other living man." Tarbell, Nationalizing of Business, 259. "Facts alone stirred his mind. No

man was ever witty enough or wise enough to impress
Nelson Dingley, but no fact was too unimportant to receive his attention." Tarbell, Tariff, 240. According
to his biographer, "Dingley's accurate knowledge of
tariff schedules, rates and classifications was the
marvel of his associates. . . . His mind was a reser-
voir of facts and figures which he marshaled as a
general marshals his soldiers—by companies and
battalions." In the preparation of this bill Dingley
utilized especially the help of Representatives Sereno
E. Payne of New York and John Dalzell of Pennsylvania. E. N. Dingley, Dingley, 418, 419. In declining
to serve as Secretary of the Treasury, Dingley indicated that in view of his physical frailty he could play
a more effective role as chairman of the Ways and
Means Committee. Dingley to McKinley, December
22, 1896, ibid., 413-14. See also Rhodes, McKinley
and Roosevelt Administrations, 38; Dunn, Harrison to
Harding, I, 313-14.

12. William McKinley, Speeches and Addresses of William
    McKinley from March 1, 1897 to May 30, 1900 (New
    York, 1900), 2-15; Public Opinion, XXII (March 11,
    1897), 293.

13. McKinley, Speeches, 5, 6-7.

14. Ibid., 13. Indicative of McKinley's congenial relations
    with Congress was the opening sentence of his first
    annual message of December 6, 1897, in which he
    stated: "It gives me pleasure to extend greeting to
    the Fifty-fifth Congress, assembled in regular ses-
    sion at the seat of Government, with many of whose
    Senators and Representatives I have been associated
    in the legislative service." Cong. Record, 55 Cong.,
    2 Sess., 2 (December 6, 1897). In regard to the Pres-
    ident's popularity see Cullom, Fifty Years, 275-76;
    Hoar, Autobiography, II, 46-47; Oberholtzer, History,
    V, 461-62; Henry L. Stoddard, As I Knew Them:
    Presidents and Politics from Grant to Coolidge (New
    York, 1927), 243-44; Paxson, op. cit., XII, 107.

15. McKinley, Speeches, 3.

16. In the lower chamber 202 seats were held by the Republicans, 130 by Democrats, and 25 by members classified as Silver Republicans and Populists. Stanwood, Tariff Controversies, II, 377. See also Oberholtzer, History, V, 459.

17. Olcott, McKinley, I, 349; Stanwood, History of Presidency, II, 3. Olcott notes that as against the 46 Senate seats filled by Republicans, 34 were held by Democrats, 5 by Populists, 3 by Independents, and 2 by Silver Party representatives. "The combined opposition," he states, "were all in favor of free silver and could count at least four Republicans to act with them." Olcott, McKinley, I, 349. See also Stanwood, Tariff Controversies, II, 377; Croly, Hanna, 275; Dunn, Harrison to Harding, I, 222.

18. See Taussig, Tariff History, 325; Olcott, McKinley, I, 348-49; Oberholtzer, History, V, 458-59; Mitchell and Mitchell, Economic History, 750.

19. For McKinley's extra session message of March 15, 1897, see Cong. Record, 55 Cong., 1 Sess., 13 (March 15, 1897).

20. Ibid., 13. The President's special session proclamation had been issued on March 6. Ibid., 13. See also Stanwood, Tariff Controversies, II, 378; Stanwood, History of Presidency, II, 4; Olcott, McKinley, I, 350; E. N. Dingley, Dingley, 422; Tarbell, Tariff, 242.

21. E. N. Dingley, Dingley, 427.

22. See Taussig, Tariff History, 327; Olcott, McKinley, I, 351; Peck, Twenty Years, 525; Shannon, Economic History, 585.

23. Cong. Record, 55 Cong., 1 Sess., 19 (March 15, 1897). Following the introduction of the bill, it was referred to the Ways and Means Committee, and to that body were appointed, in accordance with the pre-arranged

plan, Republican Representatives Dingley, Payne,
Dalzell, Hopkins (Illinois), Grosvener (Ohio), Russell
(Connecticut), Dolliver (Iowa), Steele (Indiana), John-
son (North Dakota), Evans (Kentucky), and Tawney
(Minnesota). See ibid., 20. On March 19 chairman
Dingley reported the bill to the House. Ibid., 71
(March 19, 1897). See also E. N. Dingley, Dingley,
423; Stanwood, Tariff Controversies, II, 379; Olcott,
McKinley, I, 350-51.

24. William J. Shultz and M. R. Caine, Financial Development of the United States (New York, 1937), 449. See
also Peck, Twenty Years, 524-25; Dunn, Harrison to
Harding, I, 223; Croly, Hanna, 275; Muzzey, United
States, II, 334; Stanwood, Tariff Controversies, II,
379; Appletons' Cyclopaedia, 3d s., II (1897), 207.

25. The vote was 205 to 122. See Cong. Record, 55 Cong.,
1 Sess., 557 (March 31, 1897); Stanwood, Tariff Controversies, II, 384; E. N. Dingley, Dingley, 428.

26. Cong. Record, 55 Cong., 1 Sess., 120-23 (March 22,
1897). See also E. N. Dingley, Dingley, 426-27;
Appletons' Cyclopaedia, 3d s., II, 207-209.

27. Cong. Record, 55 Cong., 1 Sess., 121. The transfer
of wool to the free list by the Democratic tariff act of
1894 had represented Cleveland's major achievement
in his struggle in behalf of the principle of free raw
materials. See supra, 50. Other articles which the
Dingley-directed Ways and Means Committee removed from the free list as constituted under the
Wilson-Gorman act were cotton-ties, cotton-bagging,
burlaps, lumber, and salt.

28. See Taussig, Tariff History, 330-31; Faulkner, Decline of Laissez Faire, 59.

29. Tarbell, Tariff, 243. See also ibid., 242.

30. Dunn, Harrison to Harding, I, 223.

31. Tarbell, Tariff, 242.

32. Ibid., 242-43.

33. Ibid., 243. The McKinley tariff rates were restored on agricultural products, glass, and earthenware. Flax and linen duties were raised above those in the act of 1890. See Stanwood, Tariff Controversies, II, 381.

34. Cong. Record, 55 Cong., 1 Sess., 124 (March 22, 1897).

35. The bill was passed by a vote of 38 to 28. See ibid., 2447 (July 7, 1897); Cullom, Fifty Years, 283; Stanwood, History of Presidency, II, 7; Stanwood, Tariff Controversies, II, 388; Taussig, Tariff History, 328; Marion Mills Miller (ed.), Great Debates in American History (14 vols., New York, 1913), XII, 357.

36. The Republican members of this committee included chairman Morrill of Vermont, Aldrich of Rhode Island, Allison of Iowa, O. H. Platt of Connecticut, Wolcott of Colorado, Jones of Nevada, and Burrows of Michigan. Coolidge, O. H. Platt, 253.

37. Cong. Record, 55 Cong., 1 Sess., 559 (April 1, 1897), 879 (May 4, 1897).

38. Foraker states, in regard to Aldrich, that "Nobody disputed his leadership but some of us did not always agree with him. When we felt compelled to differ we did so not only with much regret and great deference but always in a good-natured way that never fractured personal relations." Joseph Benson Foraker, Notes of a Busy Life (2 vols., 3d ed., Cincinnati, 1917) II, 7. According to Dunn, the ambition of Senator Elkins of West Virginia to secure membership in the Finance Committee proved futile because he had offended Aldrich by criticizing his knowledge of the tariff. See Dunn, Harrison to Harding, I, 224.

39. Cong. Record, 55 Cong., 1 Sess., 1227 (May 25, 1897). See also Public Opinion, XXII (June 3, 1897), 677-79; Stanwood, Tariff Controversies, II, 384-85; Stephen-

son, Aldrich, 142; Stanwood, History of Presidency,
II, 6; Tarbell, Tariff, 244.

40. Cong. Record, 55 Cong., 1 Sess., 1227. In regard to
the desire of Aldrich for a tariff measure sufficiently
moderate to avoid impairing negotiations with France
on the subject of international bimetallism, see
Stephenson, Aldrich, 138-41. Tarbell observes that
despite the generally downward revision of the rates
provided by the Finance Committee amendments,
these "also aimed, like the House bill, to protect
everything which asked protection." Tarbell, Tariff,
244.

41. Cong. Record, 55 Cong., 1 Sess., 1227.

42. As approved by the House and later enacted into law,
the sugar provisions called for an approximate doub-
ling of the rates on raw sugar as well as for increased
duties on refined sugar. See Taussig, Tariff History,
348-50; Ashley, Tariff History, 221; Oberholtzer,
History, V, 465.

43. Dunn, Harrison to Harding, I, 223.

44. Taussig, Tariff History, 351.

45. Tarbell, Tariff, 245. The New York Times observed
that "Aldrich's explanation of his sugar schedule. . . .
leaves unchanged the complicated rates which have
called out severe criticisms from his own party and
have excited the alarm of those Republicans who are
just now peculiarly apprehensive of the political effect of tariff favors to great trusts." Quoted in Public
Opinion, XXII (June 3, 1897), 678.

46. Stephenson, Aldrich, 142-44. The upper chamber,
Dunn states, "was not going to trust Aldrich" either
with the sugar schedule or the measure as a whole.
He "became conveniently ill, and the management of
the bill was turned over to Allison." Dunn, Harrison
to Harding, I, 223. See also Stanwood, History of
Presidency, II, 7; Sage, Allison, 269-71.

47. See Stephenson, Aldrich, 140, 142; Taussig, Tariff History, 328-35, 343-44; Dunn, Harrison to Harding, I, 223-24; Foraker, Notes, II, 16.

48. The Finance Committee contained six members from each of the major parties, thus putting Senator Jones, who was classified as a "Silver Republican," in a controlling position. Stanwood, Tariff Controversies, II, 386; Stanwood, History of Presidency, II, 6.

49. See Stanwood, Tariff Controversies, II, 386; Stanwood, History of Presidency, II, 7; Olcott, McKinley, I, 351.

50. Peck, Twenty Years, 525. See also Coman, Industrial History, 320. Oberholtzer states that "Many of the familiar charges that manufacturers and other beneficiaries had dictated duties and, indeed, framed entire schedules were bandied about, and there was too much ground for the suspicion of such interferences." Oberholtzer, History, V, 463. Although not vocal in the open discussions of the bill, newly-appointed Senator Hanna actively participated in the preparation of the schedules. Croly, Hanna, 275-76.

51. The Republican conferees for the Senate were Aldrich, Allison, O. H. Platt, Burrows of Michigan, and Jones of Nevada; those for the House were Dingley, Dalzell, Payne, Grosvenor, and Hopkins. Cong. Record, 55 Cong., 1 Sess., 2477 (July 7, 1897), 2704 (July 19, 1897); E. N. Dingley, Dingley, 433-34.

52. Tarbell, Tariff, 251; Stanwood, Tariff Controversies, II, 388-89. In the case of the sugar schedule the House conferees refused to surrender to the Senate demands for increased duties, the sugar provisions as adopted being essentially the same as those approved by the lower chamber. See E. N. Dingley, Dingley, 433, 435-36; Taussig, Tariff History, 351-52; Tarbell, Tariff, 245; Peck, Twenty Years, 527-28.

53. Cong. Record, 55 Cong., 1 Sess., 2698 (July 19, 1897).

54. Ibid., 2750 (July 19, 1897), 2909-10 (July 24, 1897).
See also Stanwood, Tariff Controversies, II, 389.

55. The average rate was raised from 40 per cent under
the Wilson-Gorman act to 57 per cent. Shannon,
Economic History, 586. See also McGrane, Economic
Development, 407; Ernest Ludlow Bogart, Economic
History of the American People (New York, 1931),
704; Coman, Industrial History, 319; Noyes, American
Finance, 269. As enacted the Dingley law provided
for the reimposition of duties on wool and hides, and
for increased rates on most textiles, raw and refined
sugar, earthenware, glassware, china, lead, tin plate,
iron and steel products, and coal. Few changes were
made in duties on pig iron, iron ore, and steel rails.
Ashley, Tariff History, 220-21; Oberholtzer, History,
V, 463-65; Tarbell, Tariff, 248-52.

56. See Statutes at Large, XXX (1897-1899), 151-213.

57. Sidney Ratner, American Taxation: Its History as a
Social Force in Democracy (New York, 1942), 223.
See also Reginald C. McGrane, "Lyman Judson Gage,"
Dictionary of American Biography, VII, 85-86; Moses
P. Handy, "Lyman J. Gage: A Character Sketch,"
Review of Reviews, XV (March, 1897), 289-300;
Public Opinion, XXII (February 4, 1897), 133. For
further indication of McKinley's view that the rates
established by the legislation of 1890 were too high,
see supra, 34.

58. "We believe," the platform declared, "the repeal of
the reciprocity arrangements negotiated by the last
Republican administration was a national calamity,
and we demand their renewal and extension on such
terms as will equalize our trade with other nations,
remove the restrictions which now obstruct the sale
of American products in the ports of other countries,
and secure enlarged markets for the products of our
farms, forests, and factories." McKee (ed.), Conventions and Platforms, 300-301; Porter (comp.),

Party Platforms, 202-203; John Tweedy, A History of
the Republican National Conventions from 1856 to
1908 (Danbury, Conn., 1910), 293.

59. In regard to the modification of McKinley's attitude
toward reciprocity, which he had opposed in 1890, see
Olcott, McKinley, II, 298; Croly, Hanna, 358. See also
N. I. Stone, One Man's Crusade for an Honest Tariff:
The Story of Herbert E. Miles, Father of the Tariff
Commission (Appleton, 1952), 6; Rhodes, McKinley
and Roosevelt Administrations, 173-74. In his final
address, delivered at the Pan-American Exposition
in Buffalo on September 5, 1901, the President declared: "The period of exclusiveness is past . . . .
Reciprocity treaties are in harmony with the spirit of
the times; measures of retaliation are not. If, per-
chance, some of our tariffs are no longer needed for
revenue or to encourage and protect our industries
at home, why should they not be employed to extend
and promote our markets abroad?" William McKinley, President McKinley's Last Speech (New York,
1901), 12. See also Nation, LXXIII (September 12,
1901), 197; Public Opinion, XXXI (September 19, 1901),
358-59.

60. See Tarbell, Tariff, 256.

61. These, selected partly with an eye toward pleasing
France in order to encourage her continued interest
in the proposal for the establishment of international
bimetallism, included wines, brandies, argols, statu-
ary, and paintings. Statutes at Large, XXX, 203-204;
Bogart, Economic History, 708; Stephenson, Aldrich,
139-41; Ratner, American Taxation, 225.

62. Ashley, Tariff History, 230.

63. Statutes at Large, XXX, 204-205.

64. Through the efforts of John A. Kasson, whom the
President appointed for the purpose of negotiating
reciprocity treaties, such agreements were reached

with France, the Argentine, Ecuador, and a number of countries of Central America and the West Indies. See Tarbell, Tariff, 256-57; Rhodes, McKinley and Roosevelt Administrations, 173; Ashley, Tariff History, 229; Shannon, Economic History, 586; United States Tariff Commission, Summary of the Report on Reciprocity and Commercial Treaties with Conclusions and Recommendations of the Commission (Washington, 1919), 27-28.

65. Cullom, Fifty Years, 374.

66. Ibid., 375. See also Stephenson, Aldrich, 168; Oberholtzer, History, V, 466-67; Taussig, Tariff History, 354; Samuel Flagg Bemis, A Diplomatic History of the United States (New York, 1950), 734; Nation, LXV (July 8, 1897), 21.

67. Muzzey, United States, II, 335.

68. Taussig, Tariff History, 358.

69. Croly, Hanna, 249, 275. Peck, who characterizes the Dingley act as an "economic monstrosity," observes that "The 'business man in politics,' of whom Senator Hanna was a type, ... knew that his own class reaped immense benefits from it, and perhaps he entertained a pious hope that it might in some way incidentally benefit the people as a whole. But his first thought was for himself alone, since this was 'business' . . . ." Peck, Twenty Years, 529.

70. Taussig, Tariff History, 358.

71. As Shannon notes, the protectionists in securing the enactment of the Dingley bill "were victorious beyond the wildest hopes of the preceding generation." Shannon, Economic History, 586. See also Muzzey, United States, II, 335; Phillips, op. cit., XL, 635-36.

72. See Tarbell, Tariff, 252.

73. See Noyes, American Finance, 269-70; Faulkner,

Decline of Laissez Faire, 22-23, 61; Bining, Economic
Life, 368. Olcott, with an apparent preference for the
generally rejected view that the Dingley tariff had
brought prosperity, states that "No fine-spun arguments of theoretical economists could overcome the
fact that prosperity had come, that it came in the wake
of the Dingley Law, that this result had been predicted
by the Republicans under the leadership of McKinley,
and that the promise of the party had been fulfilled."
Olcott, McKinley, II, 263.

74. Stanwood, Tariff Controversies, II, 390; Olcott, Mc-
Kinley, II, 263; Cullom, Fifty Years, 290. See also
ibid., 283.

SELECTED READINGS

Source Material

Governmental Publications

Congressional Globe
 41 Cong., 2 Sess.

Congressional Record
 45 Cong., 2 Sess.
 46 Cong., 2 Sess., 3 Sess.
 47 Cong., 1 Sess., 2 Sess.
 48 Cong., 1 Sess.
 49 Cong., 1 Sess., 2 Sess.
 50 Cong., 1 Sess., 2 Sess.
 51 Cong., 1 Sess., 2 Sess.
 53 Cong., 1 Sess., 2 Sess., 3 Sess.
 55 Cong., 1 Sess., 2 Sess.

House Reports
 House Report No. 1496 (Serial 2602) 50 Cong., 1 Sess.
  (April 2, 1888).

Statutes at Large of the United States of America
  XXVI (1889-1891)
  XXVIII (1893-1895)
   XXX (1897-1899)

United States Reports
 Pollock v. Farmers' Loan and Trust Co., 157 U.S. 429
  (1895).
 Pollock v. Farmers' Loan and Trust Co., 158 U.S. 601
  (1895).

United States Tariff Commission, Summary of the Report
on Reciprocity and Commercial Treaties with Conclusions and Recommendations of the Commission (Washington, 1919).

Books

Bowers, Renzo D. (comp. and ed.). The Inaugural Addresses of the Presidents (St. Louis, 1929).

Bryan, William J. The First Battle: A Story of the Campaign of 1896 (Chicago, 1896).

Cullom, Shelby M. Fifty Years of Public Service (2d ed.,
Chicago, 1911).

Foraker, Joseph Benson. Notes of a Busy Life (2 vols.,
3d ed., Cincinnati, 1917).

Hedges, Charles (comp.). Speeches of Benjamin Harrison
(New York, 1892).

Hoar, George F. Autobiography of Seventy Years (2 vols.,
New York, 1903).

Lodge, Henry Cabot. The Democracy of the Constitution,
and Other Addresses and Essays (New York, 1915).

McKee, Thomas Hudson (ed.). The National Conventions
and Platforms of all Political Parties, 1789 to 1901
(4th ed., Baltimore, 1901).

McKinley, William. A History of Tariff Legislation from
1812 to 1896, Vol. VII of Works of Henry Clay, Comprising His Life, Correspondence and Speeches, ed. by
Calvin Colton (New York, 1897).

_____ . President McKinley's Last Speech, Delivered September 5, 1901, President's Day at the Pan-American Exposition, Buffalo (New York, 1901).

_____ . Speeches and Addresses of William McKinley, from March 1, 1897 to May 30, 1900 (New York, 1900).

Miller, Marion Mills (ed.). Great Debates in American History, from the Debates in the British Parliament on the Colonial Stamp Act (1764-1765) to the Debates in Congress at the Close of the Taft Administration (1912-1913) (14 vols., New York, 1913), Vols. XII, XIV.

Porter, Kirk H. (comp.). National Party Platforms (New York, 1924).

Richardson, James D. (ed.). A Compilation of the Messages and Papers of the Presidents, 1789-1897 (10 vols., Washington, 1896-1899), Vols. VIII, IX, X.

Sherman, John. Recollections of Forty Years in the House, Senate and Cabinet: An Autobiography (2 vols., Chicago, New York, etc., 1895).

Smith, Joseph P. (comp.). Speeches and Addresses of William McKinley from His Election to Congress to the Present Time (New York, 1893).

Articles

Carnegie, Andrew. "My Experience with, and Views upon, the Tariff," Century Magazine (New York) New Series, LV (December, 1908), 196-205.

Reed, Thomas B. "Historic Political Upheavals," North American Review, CLX (January, 1895), 109-16.

Secondary Material

Books

Allen, Frederick Lewis. The Great Pierpont Morgan (New York, 1949).

Appletons' Annual Cyclopaedia and Register of Important Events. New Series, 1876-1895; Third Series, 1896-1902 (New York, 1877-1903). New Series, Vol. XIII, 1888, Vol. XVIII, 1893; Third Series, Vol. I, 1896, Vol. II, 1897, Vol. V, 1900.

Ashley, Percy. Modern Tariff History, Germany—United States—France (3d ed., New York, 1926).

Bailey, Thomas A. A Diplomatic History of the American People (4th ed., New York, 1950).

Barnes, James A. John G. Carlisle, Financial Statesman (New York, 1931).

Barry, David S. Forty Years in Washington (Boston, 1924).

Bates, Ernest Sutherland. The Story of Congress, 1789-1935 (New York and London, 1936).

Bemis, Samuel Flagg. A Diplomatic History of the United States (3d ed., New York, 1950).

Bining, Arthur Cecil. The Rise of American Economic Life (New York, Chicago, etc., 1943).

Bogart, Ernest Ludlow. Economic History of the American People (New York, London, and Toronto, 1931).

130

_____ , and Kemmerer, Donald L. Economic History of the American People (New York, London, and Toronto, 1947).

Brown, George Rothwell. The Leadership of Congress (Indianapolis, 1922).

Burdette, Franklin L. Filibustering in the Senate (Princeton, 1940).

Burton, Theodore E. John Sherman (Boston and New York, 1906).

Chamberlain, John. Farewell to Reform: The Rise, Life and Decay of the Progressive Mind in America (2d ed., New York, 1933).

Coman, Katherine. The Industrial History of the United States (rev. ed., New York, 1930).

Coolidge, Louis A. An Old-Fashioned Senator, Orville H. Platt (New York and London, 1910).

Corey, Lewis. The House of Morgan: A Social Biography of the Masters of Money (New York, 1930).

Croly, Herbert. Marcus Alonzo Hanna: His Life and Work (New York, 1912).

Dewey, Davis Rich. Financial History of the United States (8th ed., London, Bombay, etc., 1922).

_____ . National Problems, 1885-1897 (New York and London, 1907), Vol. XXIV of The American Nation: A History, ed. by Albert Bushnell Hart (28 vols., New York and London, 1904-1918).

Dingley, Edward Nelson. The Life and Times of Nelson Dingley, Jr. (Kalamazoo, 1902).

Dunn, Arthur Wallace. From Harrison to Harding: A Personal Narrative, Covering a Third of a Century, 1888-1921 (2 vols., New York and London, 1922), Vol. I.

Enke, Stephen, and Salera, Virgil. International Economics (New York, 1947).

Faulkner, Harold Underwood. American Economic History (5th ed., New York and London, 1943).

_____. The Decline of Laissez Faire, 1897-1917, Vol. VII of The Economic History of the United States (New York, 1951).

Follett, M. P. The Speaker of the House of Representatives (New York, 1896).

Ford, Henry Jones. The Cleveland Era: A Chronicle of the New Order in Politics, Vol. XLIV of The Chronicles of America Series, ed. by Allen Johnson (New Haven, Toronto, and London, 1921).

Galloway, George B. Congress at the Crossroads (New York, 1946).

Gantenbein, James W. (comp. and ed.). The Evolution of Our Latin-American Policy: A Documentary Record (New York, 1950).

Gillett, Frederick H. George Frisbie Hoar (Boston and New York, 1934).

Glad, Paul W. McKinley, Bryan, and the People (Philadelphia & New York), 1964.

Halstead, Murat. Life and Distinguished Services of William McKinley, Our Martyr President (Memorial Association Publishers, 1901).

Hamilton, Gail (pseud. Dodge, Mary Abigail). Biography of James G. Blaine (Norwich, Conn., 1895).

Hasbrouck, Paul De Witt. Party Government in the House of Representatives (New York, 1927).

Haynes, George H. The Senate of the United States: Its History and Practice (2 vols., Boston, 1938), Vol. I.

Holcombe, Arthur N. The Political Parties of Today: A Study in Republican and Democratic Politics (New York and London, 1924).

Hovey, Carl. The Life Story of J. Pierpont Morgan: A Biography (New York, 1911).

Josephson, Matthew. The Politicos, 1865-1896 (New York, 1938).

Kerr, Winfield S. John Sherman: His Life and Public Service (2 vols., Boston, 1908).

Kirkland, Edward C. A History of American Economic Life (rev. ed., New York, 1939).

Leech, Margaret. In the Days of McKinley (New York, 1959).

McCall, Samuel W. The Life of Thomas Brackett Reed (Boston and New York, 1914).

McGrane, Reginald C. The Economic Development of the American Nation (Boston, New York, etc., 1942).

Maxwell, James A. The Fiscal Impact of Federalism in the United States (Cambridge, Mass., 1946).

Mayer, George H. The Republican Party, 1854-1966 (2d ed., New York, 1967).

Mitchell, Broadus, and Mitchell, Louise Pearson. American Economic History (Boston, New York, etc., 1947).

Morgan, H. Wayne. From Hayes to McKinley: National Party Politics, 1877-1896 (Syracuse, 1969).

_____. William McKinley and His America (Syracuse, 1963).

Morison, Samuel Eliot, and Commager, Henry Steele. The Growth of the American Republic (2 vols., 4th ed., New York, 1951), Vol. II.

Muzzey, David Saville. James G. Blaine: A Political Idol of Other Days (New York, 1934).

_____. The United States of America (2 vols., Boston, New York, etc., 1924), Vol. II.

Noyes, Alexander Dana. Forty Years of American Finance: A Short Financial History of the Government and People of the United States Since the Civil War, 1865-1907 (New York and London, 1909).

_____. Thirty Years of American Finance: A Short Financial History of the Government and People of the United States Since the Civil War, 1865-1896 (New York and London, 1901).

Oberholtzer, Ellis Paxson. A History of the United States Since the Civil War (5 vols., New York, 1917-1937), Vols. II, IV, V.

Olcott, Charles S. The Life of William McKinley (2 vols., Boston and New York, 1916).

Peck, Harry Thurston. Twenty Years of the Republic, 1885-1905 (New York, 1907).

Poole, Kenyon Edwards (ed.). Fiscal Policies and the American Economy (New York, 1951).

Ratner, Sidney. American Taxation: Its History as a Social Force in Democracy (New York, 1942).

Reinsch, Paul S. (ed.). Readings on American Federal Government (Boston, New York, etc., 1909).

Ripley, Randall B. Party Leaders in the House of Representatives (Washington, 1967).

Rhodes, James Ford. History of the United States from the Compromise of 1850 (9 vols., New York, 1893-1919), Vols. VII, VIII.

_____. The McKinley and Roosevelt Administrations, 1897-1909 (New York, 1922).

Robinson, William A. Thomas B. Reed: Parliamentarian (New York, 1930).

Sage, Leland L. William Boyd Allison: A Study in Practical Politics (Iowa City, 1956).

Satterlee, Herbert L. J. Pierpont Morgan: An Intimate Portrait (New York, 1939).

Shannon, Fred Albert. Economic History of the People of the United States (New York, 1934).

Shultz, William J., and Harriss, C. Lowell. American Public Finance (5th ed., New York, 1949).

_____, and Caine, M. R. Financial Development of the United States (New York, 1937).

Stanwood, Edward. A History of the Presidency (2 vols., rev. ed., Boston and New York, 1928).

_____. American Tariff Controversies in the Nineteenth Century (2 vols., Boston and New York, 1903), Vol. II.

Steffens, Lincoln. The Autobiography of Lincoln Steffens (New York, 1931).

Stephenson, Nathaniel Wright. Nelson W. Aldrich: A Leader in American Politics (New York, 1930).

Stern, Clarence A. Golden Republicanism: The Crusade for Hard Money (Ann Arbor, 1970).

_____. Republican Heyday: Republicanism Through the McKinley Years (Ann Arbor, 1969).

_____. Resurgent Republicanism: The Handiwork of Hanna (Ann Arbor, 1968).

Stoddard, Henry L. As I Knew Them: Presidents and Politics from Grant to Coolidge (New York and London, 1927).

Stone, N. I. One Man's Crusade for an Honest Tariff: The Story of Herbert E. Miles, Father of the Tariff Commission (Appleton, Wis., 1952).

Tarbell, Ida M. The Nationalizing of Business, 1878-1898, Vol. IX of A History of American Life, ed. by Arthur M. Schlesinger and Dixon Ryan Fox (New York, 1936).

_____. The Tariff in Our Times (New York, 1911).

Taussig, F. W. The Tariff History of the United States (5th ed., New York and London, 1901).

Thompson, Charles Manfred, and Jones, Fred Mitchell. Economic Development of the United States (New York, 1939).

Tweedy, John. A History of the Republican National Conventions from 1856 to 1908 (Danbury, Conn., 1910).

Tyler, Alice Felt. The Foreign Policy of James G. Blaine (Minneapolis, 1927).

Willoughby, W. F. Principles of Legislative Organization and Administration (Washington, 1934).

Woodburn, James Albert. Political Parties and Party Problems in the United States: A Sketch of American Party History and of the Development and Operations of Party Machinery, Together with a Consideration of Certain Party Problems in Their Relations to Political Morality (New York and London, 1909).

Articles

Dunn, Arthur Wallace. "Senator Allison's Recollections of Public Men," Review of Reviews. XXXIX (May, 1909), 555-60.

Handy, Moses P. "Lyman J. Gage: A Character Sketch," Review of Reviews, XV (March, 1897), 289-300.

"Hearings on the Tariff," Nation, L (January 2, 1890), 4.

Low, A. Maurice. "The Oligarchy of the Senate," North American Review, CLXXIV (February, 1902), 231-44.

McGrane, Reginald C. "Lyman Judson Gage," Dictionary of American Biography, VII, 85-86.

"Mr. Cleveland's Letter of Acceptance," Harper's Weekly (New York), XXXVI (October 8, 1892), 962.

Needham, Henry Beach. "The Senate—of 'Special Interests,'" World's Work (New York), XI (January, 1906), 7060-65, (February, 1906), 7206-11.

Nichols, Jeannette P. "John Sherman," Dictionary of
American Biography, XVII, 84-88.

_____. "William Boyd Allison," Dictionary of
American Biography, I, 220-22.

Phillips, David Graham. "The Treason of the Senate,"
Cosmopolitan Magazine (New York), XL (April, 1906),
628-38, XLI (May, 1906), 3-12, (October, 1906), 627-36.

Robinson, William A. "Thomas Brackett Reed," Dictionary of American Biography, XV, 456-59.

"Senator Allison," Nation, LXXXVII (August 13, 1908),
132-33.

Steffens, Lincoln. "Rhode Island: A State for Sale, What
Senator Aldrich Represents—a Business Man's Government Founded upon the Corruption of the People Themselves," McClure's Magazine, XXIV (February, 1905),
337-53.

Stephenson, Nathaniel Wright. "Nelson Wilmarth Aldrich,"
Dictionary of American Biography, I, 151-58.

"Tariff-Making Extraordinary," Nation, LXIV (April 8,
1897), 256.

"The Mugwump Justification," Nation, XLVII (July 5,
1888), 4.

"The Presidency and Senator Allison," Atlantic Monthly,
LXXVII (April, 1896), 544-51.

Volwiler, Albert T. "Benjamin Harrison," Dictionary of
American Biography, VIII, 331-35.

Miscellaneous Periodical References

<u>Nation</u>, L, LI, LXV, LXXIII.

<u>Public Opinion</u>, IV, V, VII-X, XIII, XVII, XXII, XXXI.

About REPUBLICAN HEYDAY by C. A. Stern:

". . . an interesting introduction to an era. . . ." —
The American Book Collector.

". . . will quicken the hearts of life-long Republicans. . . ." — "Political Notes," — *The Cedar Rapids Gazette*.

". . . discusses the American political scene during the last decades of the 19th century, and the policy of conservatism and <u>laissez faire</u> that was firmly entranced at the century's close. This scholarly account is fully annotated, and an extensive bibliography is appended." — *The Book Exchange*.

". . . a record and critical analysis of the Republican Party during the period that William McKinley was president." — *Sioux Falls Argus-Leader*.

". . . narrative of the evolution of the Republican Party to 1901 with focus on 'the leader who contributed most decisively to the ameliorating fortunes of the party,' Senator Marcus A. Hanna of Ohio." — *Journal of Economic Literature*.

"Cette étude se concentre sur le Parti Républicain, depuis le moment où il s'est implanté solidement, tout juste après la guerre civile, en 1901, en se faisant le champion de l'industrialisme. Il profita de la situation: l'administration Harrison s'étant rendue impopulaire par ses mesures d'austérité, les autres partis s'en trouvaient fortement affaiblis et désunis. C'est alors que les principaux leaders républicains préconisèrent une politique protectionniste et impérialiste, afin de conduire la nation vers une ère de prospérité économique."—REVUE DE DROIT INTERNATIONAL, de Sciences Diplomatiques et Politiques (THE INTERNATIONAL LAW REVIEW), (Sottile-Geneve).

About RESURGENT REPUBLICANISM by C. A. Stern:

". . . the graphic story of a smooth 'king maker' in action. . . . the story of the powerful Ohio Republican leader . . . Mark Hanna. How he decided upon William McKinley to be president. . . ." —*The Sacramento Union.*

"A scholarly study of Mark Hanna's influence on the Republican party. Hanna 'elected' McKinley president in 1896 and nearly became Grand Prexy himself! Timely!"—Edwin T. Grandy, *News Features.*

"An important contribution to American political history of the late 1800s is the book RESURGENT REPUBLICANISM. . . . This book concerns the men and issues of the McKinley era. . . ." —*Annals of Iowa.*

". . . exceptionally well received. . . . a compact and authoritative account of the revitalisation of Republicanism in American politics in the closing years of last century, with its focus on the important part played by Mark Hanna. . . . Dr. Stern has fully documented his able analysis of events and personalities, and his book makes an important contribution to American political history during the closing years of the last century. A comprehensive bibliography has been included." —*The Book Exchange.*

". . . Marcus Hanna's role in the nomination of McKinley for the presidency, with some discussion of Hanna's own ambitions for that office." —*Journal of Economic Literature.*

"Ce livre décrit la plus belle période du Parti Républicain des Etats-Unis, qui connaissait un certain déclin durant la période de l'administration Harrison. En effet, les élections de 1896 sont généralement reconnues comme le triomphe de la classe des commerçants et des entrepreneurs qui allait marquer le début d'une campagne gigantesque menée par le Parti Républicain, pour l'industrialisation. Dès cette époque, les intérêts économiques et politiques furent indissolublement liés aux Etats-Unis." —REVUE DE DROIT INTERNATIONAL, de Sciences Diplomatiques et Politiques (THE INTERNATIONAL LAW REVIEW), (Sottile-Geneve).

About REPUBLICAN HEYDAY,
RESURGENT REPUBLICANISM,
and GOLDEN REPUBLICANISM
by C. A. Stern:

". . . a helpful source of writings about the men
and issues of the McKinley era. . . ." [bringing to-
gether] "in readable fashion an analysis of materials
from widely-scattered periodicals and books. . . .
useful as background works and bibliographical
sources. . . . useful evaluations of the careers of
John Sherman, William McKinley, Mark Hanna, and
other prominent Republicans of the era. . . . one of
the most interesting and revealing aspects of the
books is the analysis of the use of delaying and ob-
structive tactics in the Congress. . . . methods used
were those available only in legislative bodies, and
usually had the effect of obscuring issues rather than
sharpening them. . . ."—*The Quarterly Journal of
Speech*.

C. A. STERN, P.O. Box 1094,
Oshkosh, Wisconsin 54901

VERMONT COLLEGE
MONTPELIER, VERMONT.